THE FIRST 100 YEARS

THE FIRST

100

YEARS

DAVE SMITH   STEVEN CLARK

HYPERION
NEW YORK

ISBN 0-7868-6442-7
First Edition
10 9 8 7 6 5 4 3 2

Contents

Introduction AND Acknowledgments

The coming of a new millennium is truly a momentous occasion, one which naturally provokes a desire to look back at the accomplishments of the previous 100 years. A book on Disney's first century seemed a fitting tribute to the company's founder, Walt Disney, and his legacy, especially given that he was born in 1901, just as the 20th Century was beginning. While it would be several decades before he would have a significant impact on the world, his contributions would eventually leave a lasting impression in the hearts and minds of millions. Walt Disney started off with the creation of a likable little mouse he called Mickey and a feisty duck named Donald. The ensuing years would bring with them merchandise licensing, full-length animated features like *Snow White and the Seven Dwarfs* and *Pinocchio,* television programs, live-action movies and, of course, one of Walt's most ambitious projects, a theme park called Disneyland. After Walt's passing in 1966, the company he founded continued to grow and expand. Today, The Walt Disney Company touches virtually every aspect of the entertainment industry from publishing, hockey and baseball, television networks and educational materials to cruise ships, cable channels, retail stores and Internet websites. The innovative theme park in Anaheim, California, became the flagship for others in Florida, Tokyo and Paris. In fact, in today's global marketplace, there are few people in the world who don't know the Disney name or are not familiar with Mickey Mouse. No matter the generation, gender, race or nationality, Walt Disney and his legacy are certain to have touched everyone's life in one way or another. Therefore, we felt it appropriate, in the following pages, to highlight the memorable moments from Disney's first 100 years and try to remind readers of the important role Disney has played throughout this century.

Work on a project such as this one does not come without the input and continuous support of family, friends and co-workers. Special thanks go to Patrick Alo, Debbie Barlow, David Brown, Ingrid Chavarria, Amy Clark, David Clark, Ken and Harriett Clark, Becky Cline, Marc Cohen, Frank Conway, Kathie Delkos, Roy E. Disney, Tyson Ervin, Collette Espino, Michael Garcia, Barbara Gerald-Owens, Shelly Graham, Howard Green, Denise Greenawalt, Ivan Hall, Teri Hayt, Jeanette Janousek, Richard Jordan, Wendy Lefkon, Adina Lerner, Sean McAndrew, Kari Miller, Willis Nalle, Jon Niermann, Claudia Peters, Andrea Recendez, Russell Schroeder, Ken Shue, Design Office/San Francisco, Ed Squair, Rich Thomas, Sheree Thompson, Robert Tieman, David Van Iwaarden, Dion Vlachos, Pam Waterman, Dick Wells, Barbara Wilcox, Bob Witter, and Zelda Wong. They are all greatly appreciated for the valuable contributions they have made in the creation of this book.

DAVE SMITH
STEVEN CLARK
JULY 1999

THE FIRST 100 YEARS

"I only hope that we never lose sight of one thing—that it was all started by a mouse."

WALT DISNEY

...a man who would eventually revolutionize family entertainment was about to be born.

At the start of the 20th century, major changes were taking place around the world. In Great Britain, an era ended with the death of Queen Victoria. The vast separations between nations began to shrink as the first transatlantic telegraphic radio transmission took place. In the U.S., President William McKinley was assassinated, and Theodore Roosevelt took his place to become the nation's youngest president. Life would soon become simpler for Americans. The automobile made its first appearance on city streets, motion pictures were just coming into their own, and a man who would eventually revolutionize family entertainment was about to be born.

It had been thirty years since much of Chicago, Illinois, was destroyed by fire, and by 1901 a bustling metropolis, with a population approaching two million, was reappearing along the shore of Lake Michigan. A young married couple, Elias and Flora Disney, had moved to Chicago in 1889, with Elias taking up the trade of carpentry. The family had brought a baby son, Herbert, with them when they arrived from Florida, where they had married. Soon after, Herbert was joined by two

FLORA AND ELIAS DISNEY

WALT DISNEY'S BIRTHPLACE,
1249 TRIPP AVE., CHICAGO

brothers, Raymond and Roy. Besides building a house for themselves on Tripp Avenue, Elias worked on constructing houses for others, using plans drawn up by his wife. On Sunday, December 5, 1901, in a bedroom in the house on Tripp Avenue, a fourth son was born to Elias and Flora Disney. They named him Walter Elias Disney, with the first name chosen to honor the Disneys' preacher and friend, Walter Parr. The first hundred years of Disney had begun.

☆1902

On June 8, 1902, Elias and Flora Disney baptized their son Walter at the St. Paul Congregational Church in Chicago, and young Walter's baptismal certificate was signed by his namesake, Reverend Parr. The Disneys had been loyal members of the church for which Flora played the organ and which Elias had helped build. Occasionally, when the preacher was on vacation, Elias would even take the pulpit as a lay preacher. Four months later, Walter was bundled up and taken to a photographer, where, clad in the traditional white dress and propped up in a wicker chair, he posed for his first photograph.

☆1903

With four boys in their family, Elias and Flora longed for a daughter. Their wishes came true in December of 1903, when, the day after Walt's birthday, Flora presented her sons with a sister, Ruth Flora Disney. While

WALT'S BAPTISMAL CERTIFICATE

WALT DISNEY AT 10 MONTHS

RUTH DISNEY

RUTH AND WALTER IN CHICAGO

the parents had named the four boys in such a way as to enable their initials to form words—HAD (Herbert Arthur Disney), RAD (Raymond Arnold Disney), ROD (Roy Oliver Disney), WED (Walter Elias Disney)—they were stumped when it came to Ruth. Since they didn't care for RID or RUD, she became RFD, the initials for Rural Free Delivery. Ruth would joke about this in later years.

1904 TO 1905

While Elias and Flora Disney were busy raising their family in Chicago, Elias was becoming concerned about the effects that big-city life might be having on his children, especially the two teenagers. When some neighborhood kids were sent to prison for robbery, Elias decided that he had had enough. He was determined to move from the house on Tripp Avenue and he began a search for a more wholesome place to raise his kids.

1906 TO 1908

Elias had an older brother, Robert, who owned a farm just outside the town of Marceline, Missouri. Elias visited his brother there and realized that this was the place he had been looking for to raise his family. He felt that the farm would be healthier than the big city and farm work would be good training for the older boys. In 1906 he purchased a 40-acre farm for $3,000 and the family left Chicago for a new life. Young Walt was thoroughly entranced by his experiences on the farm, and as he helped his mother with the chores his little sister Ruth would tag along. On jaunts to the nearby woods, Walt would encounter raccoons and foxes and other animals, gaining a love for nature that would remain with him throughout his life.

Walt attempted some of his earliest artwork during these formative years. He drew on the side of the family's home with tar (which he soon regretted when the tar would not come off) and he sold his first drawing—a local doctor, Dr. Sherwood, asked Walt to draw a picture of his horse, Rupert, and paid him a nickel for his efforts.

RUTH AND WALT DISNEY

SANTA FE DEPOT, MARCELINE, MISSOURI

MAIN ST., MARCELINE, MISSOURI

☆1909 TO 1910

While most kids started school earlier, young Walt was almost eight years old before he began classes at Park School in Marceline. His mother had thought it would be more convenient if Ruth and Walt attended school together, so she held him back and gave him lessons at home until

WALT (FOURTH FROM LEFT IN FRONT ROW) IN HIS FIRST-GRADE CLASS PICTURE

Ruth was old enough to attend. In his first-grade photograph, Walt, sitting in the front row, looks to be one of the tallest boys in the class.

In 1910, Walt's father, Elias, became ill and could no longer endure the strain of working his farm. Walt's older brothers, Herb and Ray, had tired of farm work and left home for Kansas City, and Roy and Walt were too young to be of much help. Thus, it was the painful chore for the Disney family to sell their farm and livestock. Since Walt and Ruth had already started the second grade, the parents decided to rent a house downtown so the kids could finish the school year.

☆1911 to 1914

Walt had little memory of his early years in Chicago, so when the family moved to Kansas City, Missouri, in 1911, he found a vast change from the idyllic country life he had come to know and love. Now,

here he was in a bustling city, with unfamiliar sounds, sights and smells. There was a lot of excitement in the city for the nine-year-old boy, not the least of which was an amusement park. Just two blocks from the Disney residence was Fairmont Park, where Walt often peeked through the fence, wishing he had enough money to experience its untold wonders. But times were tough for the Disneys. Since Elias could not do strenuous work, he purchased a newspaper distributorship, and Roy and Walt were pressed into service as delivery boys. This job would keep Walt's spare time occupied for the next six years.

Walt and Ruth entered Benton School in Kansas City, where they were both required to repeat the second grade. Roy Disney graduated from high school and soon left home, first helping out with the harvest at his uncle's home in Kansas, then taking a job as a bank clerk in Kansas City.

RUTH AND WALT AGED ABOUT 9 AND 11

Walt continued to dabble in his drawing. In the fourth grade, his teacher required the class to draw a bowl of flowers; Walt's drawing was different from all the others. He had put faces on the flowers, and drawn the leaves as arms.

1915 TO 1916

While Walt was not an especially good student—he was often exhausted from his newspaper route and found his mind wandering during the teachers' lectures—there were instances when his creativity was apparent. On Abraham Lincoln's birthday in 1915, Walt surprised everyone by coming to school dressed as the nation's 16th president. With makeup, a fake beard, a stovepipe hat and a frock coat borrowed from his father, Walt stood in front of the class and recited the Gettysburg Address. The teacher was so impressed that she brought the principal to view the

WALT PFEIFFER AND WALT DISNEY, "THE TWO WALTS," POSING IN COSTUME

FRIENDS WALT PFEIFFER
AND WALT DISNEY

One event that would have a profound influence on Walt Disney took place in 1916. Marguerite Clark starred in a silent film version of the Grimm Brothers' fairy tale, *Snow White and the Seven Dwarfs*, and the Kansas City newsboys were invited to a special presentation of the film at the city's convention hall. Walt was entranced by the fairy tale.

In Kansas City the 15-year-old Walt, along with his sister Ruth, graduated from the seventh grade in commencement exercises at Benton School, but 1917 saw upheaval not only in Walt Disney's life, but in the world, as World War I had been raging in Europe.

Elias Disney had grown restless in Kansas City, and, desiring new challenges, purchased an interest in a jelly factory in Chicago. Rather than joining the family right away in Chicago,

presentation, and the principal proceeded to take Walt around to perform for each class in the school.

It was also at this time, as he reached his teen years, that Walt cemented a friendship with a classmate and neighbor, Walt Pfeiffer. The Pfeiffer house was a jolly place, and Walt loved to spend time there with his pal. Mr. Pfeiffer encouraged the boys, who had formed an interest in comedy from watching Charlie Chaplin films, to act for themselves. Soon they were putting on skits at school and even at amateur nights at the local vaudeville theaters, where they were sometimes billed as "The Two Walts."

Walt's interest in art had reached a point where he was able to convince his father to let him enroll in some children's Saturday art classes at the Kansas City Art Institute, in addition to his daytime studies at Benton. With these art classes, Walt was able to improve greatly on his drawing techniques.

WALT DRESSED FOR THE WINTER WEATHER

Walt spent the summer with his three brothers in Kansas City. With the help of his brother Roy, Walt was able to obtain a job as a news butcher on the railroad, selling newspapers, candy, and sodas to the train passengers. Not only did this allow Walt to indulge in his love of trains and see some new parts of the country, but it was a welcome change from his newspaper delivery route.

In the fall of 1917, Walt joined his family in Chicago and enrolled at McKinley High School. His one year there would be the last formal schooling he would receive. In addition to his daytime classes, Walt continued his drawing interest by taking night classes at the Chicago Academy of Fine Arts.

At McKinley High School, Walt Disney served as a cartoonist for the campus magazine, *The Voice*. For the first time, his drawings were appearing in print, and some of them echoed a theme that was pervading the country—the desire to win the war in Europe. Walt was anxious to rush to France to help out, but his age was a hindrance—one had to be 18 in order to join the military. Walt bided his time that summer with a sorting and delivery job for the Post Office, catching the eye of girls from McKinley for movie dates in the evenings. But within a few months, his desire to aid his country became paramount,

ROY IN NAVY UNIFORM WITH WALT

ONE OF WALT'S DRAWINGS FOR *THE VOICE*

WALT'S CARICATURES FROM HIS SCHOOL MAGAZINE

and with a friend and a little falsification of his age on his passport application, he was able to join the Red Cross.

In the midst of the training came thrilling news for the country—the Armistice had been signed on November 11. Walt was a little disappointed that he would not be going to Europe, but just before he was sent back home, a list was drawn up of 50 young men to head for France to help out as the troops were readying to come home. The 50th name on the list was Walt's.

Crossing to France on a ship named the *Vaubin*, Walt arrived just in time to celebrate his 17th birthday. To the farm boy from Missouri, this visit to Paris was awe inspiring. His duties included driving trucks and ambulances and chauffering Army officers around the countryside. Occasionally his artistic talents would be put to work, designing covers for canteen menus.

WALT AT A DRAWING BOARD
BESIDE HIS BUNK IN FRANCE

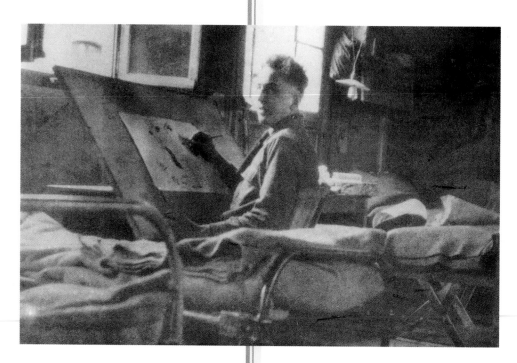

Well here I am. but no mustache —

WALT IN RED CROSS UNIFORM

☆1919

Disembarking from the ship transporting him back to America in the fall of 1919, the 17-year-old Walt Disney was a different person from the one who had left for France just a short ten months earlier. Self-assured and boasting a new maturity, Walt was full of optimism for his life, and as he made his way from New York to Chicago, he pondered his future. He had made a decision—he would become an artist. His father was not pleased with his son's choice of careers, however, and Walt felt he needed to get out of Chicago and make his way on his own.

Roy had gone back to Kansas City after being discharged from the Navy, and that is where Walt headed. He was brimming over with enthusiasm as he had a joyful reunion with his brother and spoke of his hope to get a job as a newspaper cartoonist. But,

when he applied at the Kansas City papers, he was politely turned down. Roy, however, found a way to help by suggesting Walt try the Pesmen-Rubin Commercial Art Studio. The proprietors there were intrigued by Walt's drawings of Paris, and he was hired—his first job in his newly chosen career. Walt's tasks consisted of drawing advertisements and letterheads, with one of his major clients being the Newman Theatre. Besides working on the theater's newspaper ads, he also designed the cover of their weekly program book.

A fellow artist at Pesmen-Rubin was Ubbe Iwwerks, who later would shorten his name to Ub Iwerks. Ub and Walt, being the same age, worked well together and soon became close friends. There was plenty of work to keep the two boys occupied, as stores needed advertisements for their Christmas specials. But as soon as the season was over, the work dried up and they were laid off. Even with only a few months as commercial artists, Walt and Ub, with their youthful confidence, figured that they knew enough to go into business for themselves.

NEWMAN THEATRE
MAGAZINE COVER
DESIGNED BY WALT

☆1920 TO 1921

With the dawning of the 1920s, Iwwerks-Disney Commercial Artists was formed. While Walt specialized in the cartooning, Ub handled the lettering and layout. Walt was also the salesman, pounding the pavement to drum up work for the fledgling company.

The Iwwerks-Disney partnership only lasted a month, because another opportunity came along. In an advertisement in the Kansas City *Star*, the Kansas City Slide Company (later the Kansas City Film Ad Company) noted that it was looking for an artist to do cartoon and wash drawings—"first class man wanted." Ub urged Walt to apply, and when he did, he was amazed at being offered $40 a week. A month later, Walt convinced his new boss to hire Ub as well.

At Kansas City Film Ad, Walt found a new love—animation. The company made crude, short, animated commercials for movie theaters, using the technique of stop-motion photography of cutouts that were pinned to a piece of paper and moved slightly for each frame of film. The crudeness did not satisfy Walt, so he read everything he could on real animation, which used drawings instead of cutouts.

Convincing his boss to let him borrow one of Film Ad's cameras, Walt began work during the evenings in his brother's garage on some animation of his own. Completing several minutes of a cartoon about the poor repair of Kansas City streets, he took the film to the Newman Theatre, who loved Walt's efforts and offered to buy a new cartoon every week. Not quite the savvy businessman he thought he was, Walt's hasty offer to Newman of 30 cents a foot for the cartoons just covered the costs and left no profit. But the cartoons, which he called *Newman Laugh-O-grams*, were a training ground and enabled Walt to embark on what would be his lifelong career.

Walt enjoyed life in Kansas City. He persuaded some of the young artists he met in town to help him out with

LEATHER WORKERS JOURNAL COVER BY IWWERKS-DISNEY

KANSAS CITY FILM AD SERVICE; WALT SEATED ON BRICK BALUSTER; UB IWERKS 7TH FROM THE RIGHT

WALT AT HIS DRAWING BOARD
AT KANSAS CITY FILM AD

WALT'S LETTERHEAD

his cartoon production in the garage.
He offered no pay but a promise of
better things to come.

Walt Disney and his youthful
staff spent almost half a year working
nights on their first film, a modern-
ized version of the fairy tale *Little Red
Riding Hood*. The results were promis-
ing, and Walt was able to raise enough
money selling stock to friends and rel-
atives to start up in business. Laugh-
O-gram Films was incorporated in the
State of Missouri on May 23, 1922.

Walt and his staff were thrilled
when a distributor, Pictorial Clubs,
offered to pay $11,000 for a series of
the Laugh-O-gram cartoons. They
stepped up their work, and soon had
turned out several more cartoons.
But, even though they were shipped
to Pictorial Clubs, no payments were
received for them.

LAUGH-O-GRAM
FILMS, INC. STOCK
CERTIFICATE

WALT POSES FOR HIS SECRETARY'S PHOTOGRAPHER HUSBAND

WALT AT A LAUGH-O-GRAM DRAWING BOARD

The struggling animators tried to bring in a little much-needed cash by trying a "song-o-reel," where audiences could sing along to the music of a popular song entitled "Martha." They also made an educational film on proper tooth care, called *Tommy Tucker's Tooth*, for a local dentist.

☆1923

Things were not going well in Kansas City in 1923. Money was getting scarcer and scarcer for the Laugh-O-gram staff, and most weeks the payroll could not be met. As one last ditch effort, they hired a young four-year-old model named Virginia Davis, and produced a film called *Alice's Wonderland*, in which Virginia, playing Alice, journeyed to Cartoonland. The live-action film shot of Virginia was combined with a separately produced cartoon, and the result placed Virginia within the cartoon

WALT AND VIRGINIA DAVIS IN
ALICE'S WONDERLAND

world. *Alice's Wonderland* was what we today would call a pilot film, as Walt used it to send to prospective distributors to try to interest them in a series of Alice Comedies.

It was a discouraged Walt Disney who finally decided that he would not be successful in Kansas City. He realized that if he wanted to be a success in the movie industry, he had to go where that industry was located. Surprisingly, for someone interested in animation, he did not go to New York, where all the animation studios were located, but rather headed for Hollywood. Packing his few belongings in a suitcase, he caught the train for California in July.

Besides the thought that he might give up animation and become a movie producer or director, Walt had other incentives for heading west. He had an uncle, Robert, living in Los Angeles, and his brother Roy was also there, recuperating from tuberculosis.

Writing on newly printed letterhead, Walt pursued the idea of selling his series of Alice Comedies, and, finally,

in October, he received good news. Margaret Winkler, a New York distributor of several cartoon series was willing to sign a contract for a series of Alice Comedies. But, as part of the deal, Miss Winkler wanted the same girl to play Alice. Virginia Davis's parents were willing as their roots were not deep in Kansas City, so they pulled up stakes and headed west to California. On October 16, Walt signed a contract with Miss Winkler. Not only was this the date of Walt's

(AT LEFT) VIRGINIA DAVIS WITH ANIMATED CHARACTERS IN *ALICE'S WONDERLAND;* (AT RIGHT) ANIMATED CHARACTERS CHEER FOR ALICE

WALT, HAT IN HAND, ARRIVES IN CALIFORNIA

UNCLE ROBERT DISNEY

VIRGINIA DAVIS POSES
ON A CAR

of a real estate office for his studio. He begged Roy to come and help him, and, as Roy was more or less recovered from his illness, he did so.

1924

In 1924 Walt Disney decided that he would never be a great animator. Though he had enjoyed his animation in Kansas City, he realized that there were animators who were a lot more skilled than he was, and that his own talent really lay with the story work and direction of the films. The best animator he knew was Ub Iwerks, and he soon fired off letters to Kansas City persuading Ub to come to California. Ub's arrival in June took a great deal of pressure off of Walt.

Because of the growing staff a larger space was needed, so Walt and company moved next door to the real estate office, where they had a whole office to themselves. They displayed some of their artwork underneath

first real contract, but it also marked the beginning of what is known today as The Walt Disney Company.

In Los Angeles, a couple blocks down the street from his uncle's home on Kingswell Avenue near Vermont Avenue, Walt was able to rent the back half

M. J. WINKLER
presents
a WALT DISNEY COMIC
ALICE COMEDIES
*with little
Virginia Davis*
WINKLER PICTURES

ALICE COMEDIES
LOBBY CARD

VIRGINIA DAVIS BEING PHOTOGRAPHED BY ROY AS WALT DIRECTS AND HER FATHER LOOKS ON

DISNEY BROTHERS STUDIO, which they had painted on the front window. At the end of the year, Charles Mintz, who had married Margaret Winkler and taken over her distribution business, signed a new contract with the Disney Brothers.

Alice's Day at Sea, the first Alice Comedy, was released on March 1. Others followed on a regular basis, and by the end of December, ten had been released. Walt was starting to get reviews, which he pasted in his scrapbook. "Each. . . appears to be more imaginative and clever than the preceding, and this one is a corker," wrote *Moving Picture World* about *Alice Cans the Cannibals*, and *Motion Picture News* commented that *Alice's Day at Sea* was a "novel idea. . . very unique and entertaining enough to satisfy any sort of an audience."

"Animation can

explain whatever

the mind of man

can conceive."

WALT DISNEY

There are many stories about the birth of Mickey Mouse, but the truth remains shrouded in legend...

THE NEWLYWEDS, ROY AND EDNA

LILLIAN BOUNDS AND EDNA DISNEY

1925

Roy and Walt had been living together, but they were not exactly happy with this arrangement. The two brothers got on each other's nerves, and there were frequent petty arguments. But the problem soon resolved itself when Roy decided to marry. He wired his girlfriend, Edna Francis, in Kansas City. She arrived in Los Angeles in April, and a few days later they were husband and wife. By this time, Walt had a girlfriend, too— Lillian Bounds—who had come to work for him as secretary, inker, and painter, and they attended Roy's wedding together at Uncle Robert's house on Kingswell. Perhaps to look a little more mature, Walt was now sporting a mustache, which he would retain throughout his life.

Walt soon proposed to Lillian and they were married at her brother's

WALT DECORATES A TRUCK AT ROY'S WEDDING

M. J. WINKLER
presents
ALICE'S BALLOON RACE
by Walt Disney
An ALICE Comedy
WINKLER PICTURES

COPYRIGHT MCMXXV
M. J. WINKLER

home in Lewiston, Idaho, in July of 1925. After a quick honeymoon to Mt. Rainier and Seattle, Walt returned to the Studio so that the production of the Alice Comedies would not fall behind. Virginia Davis moved on to bigger and better things, so Walt hired Margie Gay as his second Alice. A total of 15 Alice Comedies were released during the year.

☆1926

Work proceeded on the Alice Comedies at a fast pace, with 14 more being released in theaters, and the Disney Studio again outgrew its offices. In January, the move was made, not far away, to a new building

WALT AND LILLY HONEYMOONING AT MOUNT RAINIER

JOSEPH P. KENNEDY
presents

ALICE
HELPS THE
ROMANCE
by WALT
DISNEY

An ALICE Comedy
WINKLER PICTURES
A
WINKLER
PICTURE

DISTRIBUTED BY
GREATER FBO EXCHANGES EVERYWHERE

MARGIE GAY IN A
PUBLICITY PHOTO

WALT AND ROY DISNEY WITH MARGIE GAY

ALICE THE BEACH NUT POSTER ARTWORK

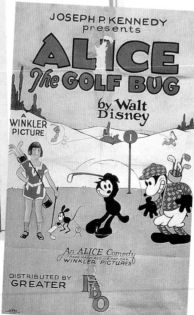

on Hyperion Avenue, in the Silver Lake area of Los Angeles. In the small building, the animators all shared a large room, and there were separate tiny offices for Walt and Roy.

By the end of the year, both Mintz and Walt were tiring of the efforts to combine live action with animation and of finding fresh new stories which would work. The novelty had worn off. For a little variety, the staff made another dental educational film for the Kansas City dentist, this one called *Clara Cleans Her Teeth*. In the meantime, Walt got his staff thinking about a new series that they could produce, and sent off to New York some sketches of a rabbit character.

☆1927

Production continued on the Alice Comedies until Spring, and the last of 17 additional titles reached movie theaters in August. But, even while they were finishing up the Alices, the Disney staff was starting work on its new series.

This new series, about a rabbit named Oswald the Lucky Rabbit, was to be made for Universal. *Trolley Troubles* was the first of the new series to be released to theaters, and again Walt was encouraged by the reception in the entertainment industry's trade papers. *Moving Picture World* said the film was "bright, speedy and genuinely amusing," while *Motion Picture News* reported that "if the first of these new cartoon comedies for Universal release is an indication of what is to come, then this series is destined to win much popular favor." Beginning in September of 1927, a new Oswald cartoon hit movie screens every two weeks.

By now, the cartoons were bringing in $2,250 each, and Walt and Roy were able to save enough money to become homeowners. They paid $7,000 each for prefabricated houses, which were built side by side on Lyric Avenue, just a few blocks from the Studio.

POOR PAPA WAS ONE OF THE FIRST OSWALD CARTOONS

OSWALD THE LUCKY RABBIT AD

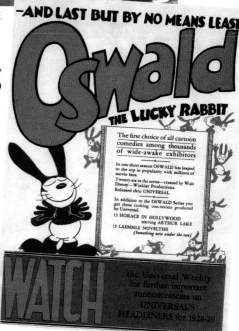

WALT'S HOME ON LYRIC AVENUE

☆1928

Walt Disney was pleased with his Oswald series, but there were problems on the horizon. When he and his wife traveled to New York in February to negotiate a contract for a second year of the Oswalds, he discovered that Mintz had signed up almost all of the animators, hoping to continue the series in his own studio without having to pay for Walt Disney and his studio's overhead. Of the primary animators, only Ub Iwerks remained loyal to Walt.

WALT DISNEY AND UB IWERKS

Walt was devastated. At first he thought he could proceed with the Oswald cartoons for another distributor, but when he studied his contract, he realized he had signed away the copyright to the distributor. This was a hard lesson for Walt to learn, but one that was very important to him. From then on, Walt would own and be very protective of everything that he ever produced. With the support of his wife and his brother Roy back home, Walt knew that he would just have to forget about Oswald, and move on to something else.

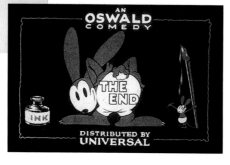

WALT DISNEY'S OSWALD SERIES ENDS

There are many stories about the birth of Mickey Mouse, but the truth remains shrouded in legend, much of it created by publicity writers and even repeated by Walt himself. The fact that Walt was discouraged and that he had to come up with a new character is evident. He probably gave it much thought on the train ride back to California, and once there he met with Ub and the few loyal staff members. Putting a drawing of Oswald on a sheet of paper, Ub was able to make some minor changes, such as substituting round ears for long ones, with a few additional modifications and—presto—there was Mickey Mouse. Of course, he was unlike any mouse anyone had ever seen. He was an "everyman" character, with Walt developing a personality for him that would endear him to audiences worldwide for generations to come.

Even while the other animators were finishing up the last of the Oswald cartoons, Ub began toiling in secret, animating the first Mickey Mouse cartoon, *Plane Crazy*, all by himself. Walt's attempts at selling the new series to a distributor, however, were unsuccessful. Walt realized he needed a novelty, and that novelty was sound. Sound had reached motion picture screens the previous fall with the release of *The Jazz Singer* by Warner Bros., and Walt decided that sound would be a great addition to animated cartoons. Ub had already finished *The Gallopin' Gaucho*, and had begun work on *Steamboat Willie* when Walt decided to make the latter as a sound cartoon. Gathering all the funds he could—even selling his car to add to the pot—he traveled to New York where he arranged to add a soundtrack to his new cartoon.

Steamboat Willie, which premiered on November 18, 1928, at the Colony Theater in New York, was the first synchronized sound cartoon, and it was a huge success. Reviewers commented on the cleverness of the cartoon, the advantage that sound brought to the medium, and the fun personality of Walt Disney's new character, Mickey Mouse. As soon as success was assured, Walt embarked on an entire Mickey Mouse series. A star was born!

PLANE CRAZY

THE GALLOPIN' GAUCHO

STEAMBOAT WILLIE

MICKEY'S FOLLIES

MICKEY MOUSE

HERE TODAY!

☆ 1929

Mickey Mouse took the world by storm. Theater audiences were disappointed when a Mickey Mouse cartoon did not accompany their feature film. "What, no Mickey Mouse?" soon would become a common expression and the title of a popular song. Walt and his staff were a bit taken aback by the overwhelming acceptance of the cartoons, but they pushed to get more of them out on a regular release schedule. Titles included *The Opry House, The Barnyard Battle, The Karnival Kid* (in which Mickey said his first words), *Mickey's Follies* (which introduced Mickey's theme song, "Minnie's Yoo Hoo"), *The Plow Boy* (in which Horace Horsecollar and Clarabelle Cow were introduced), and *The Jazz Fool.*

With the continuing success of the Mickey Mouse cartoons, Walt decided to begin a second series. Carl Stalling, who had joined the Disney Studio as composer, persuaded Walt

that a series of cartoons based on musical themes, rather than the continuing cast of characters as in the Mickey shorts, would be popular and would diversify the Studio's output. Thus, the Silly Symphonies were born—*The Skeleton Dance* being the initial offering. Five Silly Symphonies, with titles such as *Hell's Bells, The Merry Dwarfs,* and *Springtime,* joined the eleven Mickey cartoons completed during the year.

One day, Walt was walking through a hotel lobby in New York, when a man came up to him and offered him $300 if Walt would allow him to use Mickey Mouse on the cover of a children's writing tablet that he was manufacturing. Walt agreed, and thus began Mickey Mouse merchandising. Other offers soon followed, and the Disneys set up a subsidiary, Walt Disney Enterprises, to handle licensing.

Because they had invested a large amount of money in sound recording equipment for their cartoons, the Disney brothers looked for means of getting some of that money back. One

way they did this was to outfit a truck with sound equipment and provide sound recording services to other motion picture companies. For this, another subsidiary, the Disney Film Recording Company, was formed.

As one way to help promote the Mickey Mouse cartoons, the Fox Dome Theater in Ocean Park, California, decided to establish a Mickey Mouse Club for the kids who attended the weekly screenings. This idea really caught on, and soon there were Mickey Mouse Clubs springing up in theaters all around the country.

At the end of the year, it was amazing to see how different the outlook was for the Disneys from what it had been just a year earlier. Now, they had two successful cartoon series, a thriving sound recording business, and the beginnings of a major character merchandising program. They were able to expand their studio to house the increasing number of artists who were added to the payroll. All this came at the same time as the United States, along with the entire world, was pushed into the Great Depression with the stock market crash of October 1929.

☆1930

As Mickey Mouse licensing became a major business for the Disney Studio, this year saw several firsts. The first Mickey Mouse comic strip appeared in newspapers, syndicated by King Features. Bibo and Lang published the first Mickey

FIRST MICKEY MOUSE MERCHANDISE ITEM, A TABLET

© 1930—WALTER E. DISNEY

MICKEY MOUSE CLUB AT THE FOX DOME THEATER

THE DISNEY FILM RECORDING CO. PROVIDED ADDITIONAL DIVERSIFICATION FOR WALT'S COMPANY IN 1929.

FIRST MICKEY MOUSE NEWSPAPER COMIC STRIPS

WALT POSING WITH
MICKEY MOUSE DOLLS
MADE BY CHARLOTTE
CLARK

Mouse book, and Mickey's theme song, "Minnie's Yoo Hoo," became the first Disney song to be published on sheet music. In Burbank, a lady named Charlotte Clark made the very first Mickey Mouse doll; Walt was so pleased when he saw it that he set her up in business to manufacture a number of the dolls so he could use them for promotional purposes.

New Mickey Mouse cartoons such as *The Gorilla Mystery*, *The Cactus Kid*, *The Fire Fighters*, *The Shindig*, and *The Picnic*, boasted more elaborate stories and, as the artists gained more experience, improved animation. Of the nine Mickey cartoons made and now released by Columbia, one was especially notable. In *The Chain Gang* two bloodhounds were

"MINNIE'S YOO HOO" SHEET MUSIC

THE FIRE FIGHTERS

utilized to chase an escaped convict. Walt found the unnamed bloodhounds appealing, and decided to create a new character based on them. Meanwhile, at the Lowell Observatory in Flagstaff, Arizona, astronomer Clyde Tombaugh made headlines with the discovery of a distant new planet, which he named Pluto. Within a year, Walt Disney's new dog character would also become known as Pluto.

While Walt and Lilly had hoped to start a family, it was Roy and Edna who became the first to announce a happy event. Roy Edward Disney was born on January 10, 1930. Naturally, grandparents Elias and Flora Disney up in Portland were thrilled.

☆1931

The Disney animation staff was getting procedures down to a science, and the cartoons continued to appear every two or three weeks. Of the twelve Mickey Mouse cartoons released in 1931, one, *Mickey's Orphans*, became the first Disney car-

toon to receive an Academy Award nomination. In *The Moose Hunt*, Pluto was finally pegged with his new name, and he actually said two words ("Kiss me") for the first and only time in a cartoon. Among ten Silly Symphonies was one—*The Ugly Duckling*—that would become famous in a color remake eight years later.

Mickey Mouse merchandise continued to appear in stores, much of it through a license signed the previous

MICKEY'S ORPHANS

29

TOY and SPECIALTY Items

THAT HAVE BECOME THE FAVORITES
OF MILLIONS--ADULTS AND CHILDREN

Retailing from 5c. to $5.50 per piece

We also handle Mickey and Minnie Mouse Figures of

SATEEN	CELLULOID	WOOD PULP
FELT	METAL	VELVET	BISC

In Different Sizes

MICKEY AND MINNIE MOUSE

RATTLES	FUR JUMPING MICKEY
SPORT BALLS	CRICKETS
HURDY GURDY	
ROLY POLY	TOY TEA SETS
SWING	SOMERSAULTING MICKEY

The following specialties are both useful and attractive

MICKEY & MINNIE MOUSE ORCHESTRAS
ASH TRAYS, TOOTH BRUSH AND OTHER HOLDERS
New items being added to this list constantly

GEO. BORGFELDT & CO.
44-60 East 23rd Street, New York City

GEORGE BORGFELDT & CO. AD FOR MICKEY AND MINNIE MERCHANDISE

WALT CHECKS OUT MICKEY'S ADVENTURES

THE ADVENTURES OF MICKEY MOUSE (MCKAY)

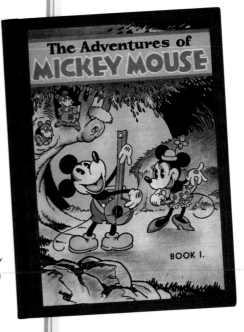

year with George Borgfeldt & Company of New York. Borgfeldt sold toys and novelties, including Mickey sparklers and acrobatic figures, many of which were manufactured in Japan. David McKay of Boston published the first hardcover Disney book, entitled *The Adventures of Mickey Mouse*, and it was a huge seller.

All this should have made Walt a very happy man, but even with the seeming success the Disney brothers could not get out of debt. Walt was a tireless worker, and he was constantly striving to make his cartoons better and better. He pushed his staff and he pushed himself, and it led to a nervous breakdown. On doctor's orders, Walt and Lilly took a long trip, heading first to Washington, D.C., to see the sights of the capital, then traveling by ship to Havana and back to California by way of the Panama Canal. The trip was a godsend for Walt and he was totally relaxed by the time he returned. He joined the Hollywood Athletic Club and took up golf and horseback riding. In December, he celebrated his 30th birthday.

✩1932

Other studios had been experimenting with color in cartoons, but Walt Disney had resisted. Then, Technicolor came out with their three-color process which enabled a film to look realistic—utilizing all the colors of the rainbow. After convincing Roy that a color cartoon would make a huge impact on audiences and be worth the extra cost, he scrapped the footage already shot of a Silly Symphony, *Flowers and Trees*, and reshot the cartoon in color. Since he was taking a big chance with the expensive process, he convinced Technicolor to give him a two-year exclusive on the use of the process for cartoons, a move which would put him well ahead of the other animation studios for years to come.

In 1932 The Academy of Motion Picture Arts and Sciences decided to include a Best Cartoon category for the first time, and at the ceremonies which were held at the Biltmore Hotel in Los Angeles in November, Walt Disney walked away with the award for *Flowers and Trees,* reinforcing his belief in the value of color. He was also presented with an honorary Oscar® for the creation of Mickey Mouse. These awards were firm acknowledgment from the industry that Walt was now one of their own.

In merchandising, an individual came along who would revolutionize the Mickey Mouse products. His name was Kay Kamen, and he was a major promoter. He convinced Walt and Roy

FLOWERS AND TREES

WALT WITH HIS FIRST OSCAR

WALT DISNEY WITH KAY KAMEN

Mickey Mouse

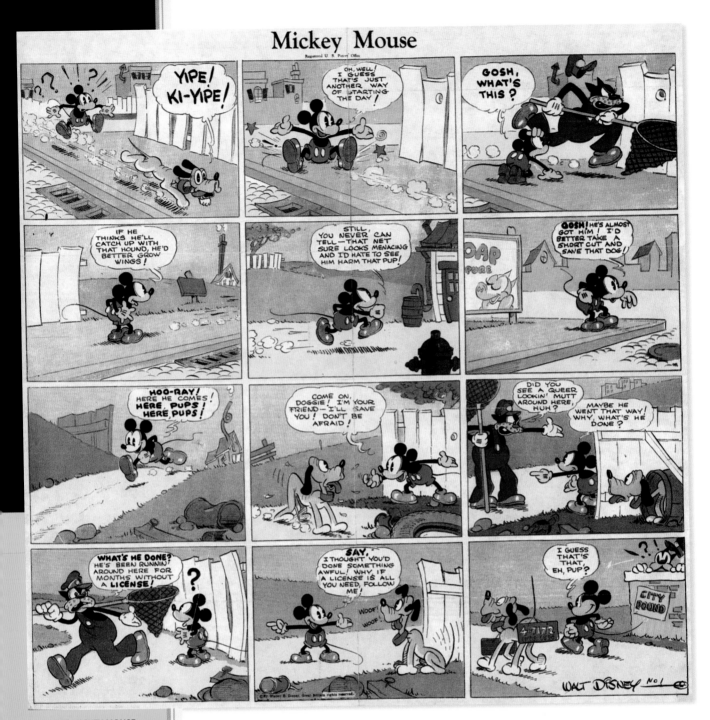

FIRST MICKEY MOUSE SUNDAY NEWSPAPER COMIC STRIP

that if he was handling the licensing, the company's merchandising revenue would greatly increase. Kamen took over the merchandising effort, and immediately set about to sign up only the best companies for each type of product, and to ensure that the licensees practiced strict quality control.

The daily Mickey Mouse comic strip in newspapers had been so successful, that in 1932 a color Sunday half-page

was begun. The success of Mickey abroad led to the first Disney periodical publication—*Topolino*—which was published in Italy at the end of the year.

In the theaters, 22 more cartoons were released, fourteen of them starring Mickey Mouse. Unsatisfied with his deal with Columbia, who had been distributing the cartoons, Walt signed a new deal with United Artists on much better terms. The cartoons had titles such as *Mickey's Good Deed, Mickey in Arabia, Trader Mickey, The Wayward Canary,* and *The Whoopee Party.* In one cartoon, *Mickey's Revue,* a minor doglike character guffawing in the audience would catch the fancy of Walt, and that character, first known as Dippy Dawg, would eventually evolve into Goofy.

As Walt had learned from his own problems the previous year, all work and no play was bad for the staff. He encouraged baseball games on a field next to the Studio, and convinced a number of the artists to join him in a new love—polo. He bought a string of ponies and participated in early morning practices before it was time to head to the Studio. Soon the Disney polo players began competing in matches often finding themselves up against celebrities such as Jack Holt, Spencer Tracy, Will Rogers, and Darryl F. Zanuck.

MICKEY'S REVUE FEATURING DIPPY DAWG (CENTER)

"WHAT! NO MICKEY MOUSE?"
SHEET MUSIC PUBLISHED

WALT ASTRIDE HIS POLO PONY

BUILDING A BUILDING

THREE LITTLE PIGS

"WHO'S AFRAID OF THE BIG
BAD WOLF?" SHEET MUSIC

☆1933

The popularity of Mickey
Mouse seemed to have no bounds. By
1933, Walt Disney and his character
were well known throughout the
world. Twelve more Mickey cartoons
were made, with the character continuing to be portrayed in a number of
professions. In *Building a Building*, he
operated a steamshovel; in *Mickey's
Mellerdrammer*, he was an actor; and
in *The Steeplechase*, he was a jockey.
Mickey's Gala Premiere was the first
Disney cartoon to caricature a large
group of Hollywood personalities.

The big breakthrough came with the
year's third Silly Symphony (out of
seven). Choosing an old fairy tale,
Walt and his staff began work on
Three Little Pigs. All of the expertise
in coming up with a succinct story
and giving well-rounded personalities
to the characters reached a pinnacle
in this film, and when it was released
it became a sensation. The time was
right for such a cartoon—Americans,

still deep in the Great Depression, were trying to keep the "Big Bad Wolf" away from their own doors, so the plight of the little pigs hit close to home. The song, "Who's Afraid of the Big Bad Wolf?" was released on sheet music and became a sort of rallying cry by people trying to beat the Depression. The film became one of the most popular shorts of all time, and justly was honored with an Academy Award.

The most famous Mickey Mouse merchandise item of all time was created in the spring when Ingersoll was licensed to come out with a Mickey Mouse watch. Both wristwatch and pocket watch styles were made, and they were a big hit. In publishing, Kay Kamen created the first Mickey Mouse magazine in the U.S., with the first version being distributed monthly by dairies.

INGERSOLL MICKEY
MOUSE WATCH

ELIAS AND FLORA
DISNEY HOLDING
BABY DIANE

At the end of the year, Walt and Lilly Disney finally presented Roy Edward with a cousin. Diane Marie Disney was born on December 18. The Disneys had also just moved into a new, English Tudor–style home that they had built on Woking Way in the Los Feliz hills of Los Angeles.

1934

Pluto and Goofy had already joined Horace Horsecollar and Clarabelle Cow in the Mickey Mouse cartoons, but another character who would eventually eclipse them all was about to be born. As part of a 1934 Silly Symphony entitled *The Wise Little Hen*, Walt included two bit players. One was Peter Pig; the other was Donald Duck. It was the first and only role for Peter Pig, a character who shall forever live in obscurity, but for Donald Duck it was just beginning. The duck's voice was supplied by Clarence Nash, and even

WRITTEN AND ILLUSTRATED BY THE STAFF OF THE WALT DISNEY STUDIOS

ORPHAN'S BENEFIT

GRASSHOPPER AND THE ANTS

though people said they could not understand the character, they nevertheless fell in love with him. The animators and storymen were also entranced with this wacky, volatile duck, and they found it easy to write situations for him in the cartoons. So, Donald moved out of the Silly Symphonies and became part of Mickey's gang, first appearing with him in *Orphan's Benefit.*

Some of the most classic of all the Silly Symphonies came out in 1934. One, *Grasshopper and the Ants,* was an entertaining fable with another popular song—"The World Owes Me a Living."

Walt Disney had come to realize that income from the shorts kept his company going, but there was no real money to be made. To achieve any type of financial wealth, he would have to make a feature film. It was

decided that the story which had intrigued him since he saw the live action version of the tale as a Kansas City newsboy, *Snow White and the Seven Dwarfs*, would be the company's first animated feature film. He sat his artists down in the Studio's sound stage one evening and told them the story of Snow White. The performance must have been electric, because everyone who was in attendance came out of the meeting thoroughly convinced that they could indeed make an animated feature, despite what the critics would say.

Over in France, *Le Journal de Mickey* began publication, and in the U.S., the *Mickey Mouse Waddle Book*, one of the more inventive publications featuring the character, was

released. Mickey and the other characters were to be punched out of the book and assembled in such a way that they could waddle down a supplied ramp. In merchandise, a popular Mickey Mouse/Minnie Mouse railroad handcar managed to save the Lionel company from bankruptcy.

WALT PLAYING WITH THE *WADDLE BOOK*

MICKEY MOUSE HANDCAR MADE BY LIONEL

37

MICKEY MOUSE CARTOONS
ADD COLOR

THE TORTOISE AND THE HARE

THREE ORPHAN KITTENS

DONALD DUCK
MERCHANDISE

★1935

As preliminary work was being done on *Snow White and the Seven Dwarfs*, the cartoon shorts were in better shape than ever. 1935's *The Band Concert* marked the first color Mickey Mouse cartoon, and soon all of the Disney cartoons were multi-hued. Because of the Academy's qualifying year, two of the Silly Symphonies released during 1935 won Academy Awards—*The Tortoise and the Hare* and *Three Orphan Kittens*. The year also saw a Mickey Mouse balloon added to Macy's Thanksgiving Day Parade in New York City. And scores of Donald Duck merchandise items began joining Mickey Mouse and Three Little Pigs products in stores.

To celebrate their tenth wedding anniversaries, and because Walt was again getting overworked and overstressed, Roy convinced him that they should take their wives on a lengthy vacation to Europe. In Paris, Walt was presented with a medal by the League of Nations.

☆1936

There was a tremendous surge of energy around the Disney Studio as work on *Snow White and the Seven Dwarfs* reached a feverish pace. Regular story meetings were held, during which the elements of the film were discussed in great detail.

While most of the key animators and other staff were busy on the feature, others continued the steady stream of shorts. There were nine Mickey Mouse cartoons, including *Mickey's Polo Team* (which used caricatures of Hollywood stars to spoof Walt's new hobby), *Mickey's Grand Opera*, *Thru the Mirror* (putting Mickey in an *Alice Thru the Looking Glass* story), *Alpine Climbers*, and *Moving Day* (with its story about eviction again providing a reference to the Depression). But, interestingly, the

ANIMATOR DICK LUNDY
DRAWS A DWARF

INKER FERN AHLSTRAND OUTLINES
SNOW WHITE

MOVING DAY

THRU THE MIRROR

tenth Mickey Mouse cartoon in the series did not star Mickey Mouse. *Donald and Pluto* marked Donald Duck's first starring role. Soon he would have his own cartoon series.

The Silly Symphonies continued, with *The Country Cousin* winning the Best Cartoon Oscar.

Honors continued to pour into the Disney Studio. One of the most prestigious came when Walt was inducted into the French Legion of Honor. In England, the *Mickey Mouse Weekly* began publication. And, at the end of 1936, Walt and Lilly's second daughter, Sharon, was born.

1937

At the dawning of 1937, United Artists was still distributing the Disney cartoons, but by September that would change, when RKO took over the task. Since the Silly Symphonies had essentially served as a training ground for those who would go on to work on *Snow White* and subsequent animated features, the series was slowly coming to a halt as the training element was no longer needed. Only three Silly Symphonies were released during the year—*Woodland Cafe, Little Hiawatha,* and *The Old Mill.*

The last of the three, *The Old Mill,* featured a major breakthrough by the Disney staff—it was the first film to utilize the multiplane camera. Engineered by Disney technician Bill Garity, the camera photographed layers of backgrounds painted on glass to provide the illusion of depth. The film would win an Academy Award for Best Cartoon, and the camera itself would win a technical Oscar for the staff.

In the Mickey Mouse cartoons, Walt Disney found a pattern that was most successful—casting Mickey Mouse,

WALT RECEIVING THE LEGION OF HONOR MEDAL FROM THE FRENCH CONSUL

(AT LEFT) *LITTLE HIAWATHA;* (AT RIGHT) *WOODLAND CAFE*

Donald Duck, and Goofy together. Known as "the gang," the three starred in six of this year's seven Mickey cartoons—*Magician Mickey, Moose Hunters, Mickey's Amateurs, Hawaiian Holiday, Clock Cleaners,* and *Lonesome Ghosts*—films praised by many as some of the best Mickey Mouse cartoons of all. As had happened the previous year in 1936, two additional "Mickey Mouse cartoons"

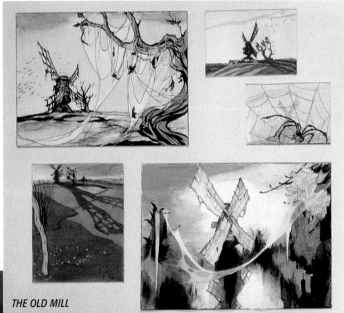

THE OLD MILL

THE MULTIPLANE CAMERA

CLOCK CLEANERS

HAWAIIAN HOLIDAY

DON DONALD

LONESOME GHOSTS

PLUTO'S QUIN-PUPLETS

appeared, starring Donald instead of Mickey—*Don Donald* and *Modern Inventions*. In the former, a winsome señorita named Donna made her debut; eventually she would be renamed Daisy Duck. These cartoons established Donald Duck as a star in his own right, and the next cartoon, *Donald's Ostrich*, would be the first to be labeled a Donald Duck cartoon. Pluto also became a star on his own, starring in *Pluto's Quin-Puplets*, the first of 48 that he would make over the next 14 years.

Walt Disney's *Snow White and the Seven Dwarfs* received a big gala premiere at the Carthay Circle Theater in Hollywood on December 21. Walt Disney himself was thrilled that a film of his could receive this kind of a Hollywood welcome. Basking in the glory, he stepped up to the microphone and was so flustered that he could not remember the names of the Seven Dwarfs.

Immediately after the premiere, it was obvious that *Snow White* was going to be a major success. Walt Disney now knew that animated features would be the Disney Studio's key to the future. It was hard for him to realize that it had been only nine short years since a crudely drawn mouse named Mickey had debuted in *Steamboat Willie*. There had probably been more advances in the Disney craft in those nine years than would occur for decades to come.

WICKED QUEEN FROM *SNOW WHITE AND THE SEVEN DWARFS*

(AT LEFT) SLEEPY FROM *SNOW WHITE AND THE SEVEN DWARFS*; (BELOW) SNOW WHITE AND FOREST ANIMALS

FIRST MOVIE
SOUNDTRACK ALBUM

✫1938✫

The impact of *Snow White and the Seven Dwarfs* was amazing. It opened at Radio City Music Hall in New York City, and soon, all around the country. Everyone seemed to be whistling the songs. RCA Victor rushed out a soundtrack album early in the year; in fact it was the first movie album ever to be produced utilizing the actual soundtracks recorded for the movie. Kay Kamen pulled a masterful merchandising coup. *Snow White* was the first film ever to have a complete merchandising campaign in place on the day the movie opened. Theatergoers could rush right down to their local Woolworth's or Sears and buy a *Snow White* memento. *Snow White* would at one point become the highest-grossing film of all time.

Under pressure to expand his staff, Walt Disney also knew that he would have to expand his Studio, but he had run out of space on Hyperion Avenue. So, looking afield, he found a plot of land the right size just over the hills in Burbank and put a deposit on the property.

A trend was beginning in the shorts. There were five Mickey cartoons released (including the Academy Award-nominated *Brave Little Tailor*, the most expensive cartoon Disney had made up to that time), but there were seven Donald Duck cartoons. Already, animators were finding that Donald, with his wild personality, was an easier character to work with.

BRAVE LITTLE TAILOR

DONALD DUCK WITH HIS NEPHEWS IN A STORY SKETCH FROM *GOOD SCOUTS*

Mickey Mouse had settled into a rut; Donald offered many more possibilities. Never again would Mickey Mouse be the preeminent character in the Disney stable. One of the Donald cartoons, *Donald's Nephews*, brought Huey, Dewey, and Louie to the screen for the first time (they had made their actual debut the previous year in a newspaper comic strip.) In order to try to revive Mickey's popularity, animator Fred Moore redesigned him with Walt's approval, softening the shapes, bulging out the cheeks a bit, and creating a more expressive eye—a white oval with a black pupil.

The Best Cartoon Oscar for the year would be won by a film that had started out as a Silly Symphony but was eventually released as a special cartoon—*Ferdinand the Bull*. Taken from the popular book by Munro Leaf, the film became a favorite with audiences everywhere.

Elias and Flora Disney celebrated their 50th wedding anniversary with their children, and decided to move to Southern California to be nearer to Walt and Roy and their growing families. But the brothers were devastated late in the year when their mother suddenly passed away.

1939

Because of the intense public acceptance of *Snow White and the Seven Dwarfs*, the Academy of Motion Picture Arts and Sciences realized that it had been remiss during the previous year's ceremonies, when the

THE DISNEY FAMILY CELEBRATES ELIAS AND FLORA'S 50TH WEDDING ANNIVERSARY

45

WALT DISNEY RECEIVES SPECIAL *SNOW WHITE* OSCAR
FROM SHIRLEY TEMPLE

SOCIETY DOG SHOW

THE POINTER

animated feature did not receive an award. So, belatedly, at the 1939 ceremony, Shirley Temple was called upon to present Walt Disney with a special Academy Award for *Snow White*. It consisted of one full-size Oscar and seven smaller Oscars on a specially built wooden pedestal.

Things were jumping at the Disney Studio on Hyperion Avenue. Not only were there several features in production, but a full quota of shorts was being prepared for theaters. Mickey starred in only two cartoons, *Society Dog Show* and *The Pointer*. The latter received an Oscar nomination and was the first to show off the newly designed Mickey. Two Silly Symphonies brought that series to an end, with *The Practical Pig*, the final of three sequels to *Three Little Pigs*, and *The Ugly Duckling*, a color remake of a 1931 Silly Symphony. *The Ugly Duckling* would win the year's Best Cartoon Oscar.

There was a new addition to the Disney cartoon series—Goofy now had his own. The first Goofy cartoon was *Goofy and Wilbur*, in which Goofy's grasshopper pal literally becomes live bait when the pair goes fishing.

1939 also saw the arrival of ominous news from Europe, as Hitler invaded Poland in September, followed by Britain and France declaring war on Germany. The beginning of World War II would have a major impact on the Disney Studio over the next decade, as it would all across America and around the globe.

Construction continued throughout the year in Burbank, as workmen hurried to finish the buildings at the new Disney Studio. Walt Disney closely supervised the work—for he wanted an ideal place for his animators. He had chosen Kem Weber, a proponent of art moderne, as architect for the Studio beginning a Disney tradition of steering away from the norms in architecture. Most of the construction was completed by the end of the year, and the move from Hyperion Avenue began during the last week in December.

WALT DISCUSSES PLANS FOR HIS NEW ANIMATION BUILDING

THE DISNEY STUDIO MOVES TO BURBANK

DISNEY THE FIRST 100 YEARS **47**

PINOCCHIO WITH
STROMBOLI, AN
EARLY PAINTING BY
GUSTAV TENGGREN

WALT WITH *PINOCCHIO* MODELS

☆1940

Moving the entire Disney
Studio to Burbank made it difficult
to concentrate on work. But such
concentration was necessary, because
two feature-length motion pictures
were nearing completion.

The first, *Pinocchio*, had essentially
been completed at the Hyperion
Studio. Only the final finishing
touches had to be added so that the
film could make its premiere in New
York City on February 7. The tale of
the little wooden puppet who wanted
to be a real boy was hailed by critics
as a masterpiece of animation. Not
only was there a clear, succinct story,
but the techniques utilized by the
animation staff had progressed by
great bounds since *Snow White*, a
little over two years earlier. But, the
advances in *Pinocchio* had not come
cheaply; the film ended up costing

almost twice that of its predecessor. Those high costs came at a time when the Disney Studio was beginning to feel financial pressures, the most significant being the loss of European markets due to the start of the war.

A second animated feature, *Fantasia*, was also well into production as the year began. It had actually begun two years earlier as a short, *The Sorcerer's Apprentice*, animated to the music of Paul Dukas, conducted by Leopold Stokowski. Because of the additional effort put into the film—not to mention the costs of the symphony orchestra and the conductor—Roy and Walt Disney realized that they could never make their costs back if they released it as a short. Thus began the idea of doing an entire "Concert Feature," as the film was known dur-

ing production, where a group of classical pieces would be combined with Disney animation. *Fantasia* premiered at the Broadway Theater in New York on November 13—the same theater, previously known as the Colony, where *Steamboat Willie* had opened a short dozen years earlier almost to the date.

THE SORCERER'S APPRENTICE SEQUENCE FROM *FANTASIA*

FANTASIA SKETCH

WALT DISNEY'S COMICS
AND STORIES, NO. 1

With the growing acceptance that the Disney output qualified as art, the Los Angeles County Museum opened a retrospective exhibit of Disney animation. In publishing, the *Mickey Mouse Magazine* founded by Kay Kamen years earlier evolved into a comic book, with the release of *Walt Disney's Comics and Stories* #1 in October of 1940.

This was the first year since the beginning of the Academy Awards for Best Cartoon that a Disney cartoon was not among the nominations. The award would be won by MGM's *The Milky Way*.

1941

The euphoria at the Disney Studio was wearing off. While *Snow White and the Seven Dwarfs* had been a spectacular box office success, neither *Pinocchio* nor *Fantasia* was able to come anywhere close. The war raging in Europe was having greater and greater consequences on America, and the Disney Studio was feeling them.

Walt Disney knew that his business would have to change in order to weather the difficult times. He believed that animation could be used to help the war effort, and in cooperation with Lockheed Aircraft, the Disney Studio made an educational film, *Four Methods of Flush Riveting*, which utilized animation to demonstrate processes that could never have been depicted in live action. The

WORLD WAR II BRINGS MILITARY WORK TO THE DISNEY STUDIO

Disney artists also began turning out hundreds of insignias, featuring the Disney characters and specially designed mascots, to raise the morale of the fighting units.

INSIGNIA FOR 144TH F.A. BATTERY, FT. LEWIS, WASHINGTON

Because of the war it was necessary to cut costs drastically. First, Disney rushed out a modest film, *The Reluctant Dragon*, which served several purposes—it got a feature film out into the theaters to hopefully help the cash flow, it kept the staff busy, and it answered a common request to show off some of the processes used in making animated films at the Disney Studio. The film combined a live-action story, featuring humorist Robert Benchley touring the Disney Studio, with cartoon segments. The feature included a Goofy cartoon, *How to Ride a Horse*, which began a lengthy series of popular "How to" short cartoons featuring Goofy trying to demonstrate the correct way to do something and never quite being able to get it right.

Work also progressed on the next animated feature, *Dumbo*, which was ready for release in October. *Dumbo* told the charming tale of a baby circus elephant with one apparent flaw—tremendously over-sized ears. With cost-cutting, *Dumbo* was only 64 minutes long, enabling it to come in at only slightly over $800,000, but critics and the general public loved it, and it brought in some much-needed cash.

THE RELUCTANT DRAGON

LITTLE HIAWATHA INSIGNIA FOR 77TH BOMBARDMENT SQDN., BOISE AIR BASE, IDAHO

GOOFY IN *HOW TO RIDE A HORSE*

INSIGNIA FOR 134TH MEDICAL REGIMENT, 2D BATT., FT. BRAGG, NC

TIMOTHY MOUSE WITH DUMBO

Nelson Rockefeller, who was Coordinator of Inter-American Affairs in the State Department, came to Walt Disney with a proposal to go on a goodwill tour of South America. The U.S. government was worried about the increasing Nazi influence on its neighbors to the south, and Mr. Rockefeller reasoned that Walt would be an excellent ambassador because of the popularity of the Disney cartoons south of the border. A hand-shaking tour did not appeal to Walt, but he did agree to take some of his artists to selected Latin American countries and prepare some cartoon segments about those countries. The tour was a grand success, and would lead to two features with Latin American themes over the next few years.

At the same time that Walt and his artists were soaking up the culture in South America, a union problem that had been festering at the Disney Studio evolved into a bitter strike. The strike, over wages and union representation, would cause strained feelings among Disney staff members for years to come and would forever change the atmosphere on the Studio lot.

As the year was coming to a close, the war finally had a direct effect on the United States, with the country becoming a combatant after the bombing of Pearl Harbor. As the U.S. entered the war, the Army, needing more space for operations, moved onto the Studio lot in Burbank, using parking sheds for storage and repairing military vehicles inside the sound stage. Work began almost immediately on training films for the military, many on top-secret subjects. Disney staff members were fingerprinted and had to show special IDs to get onto the lot. The rigors of war would affect the Disney Studio's output for the next four years.

WALT DONS GAUCHO GARB IN SOUTH AMERICA

WALT POSES FOR A PORTRAIT

STRIKE AT THE DISNEY STUDIO

☆1942

With American servicemen being sent overseas, Americans at home found their everyday lives influenced more and more by the war. Some Disney cartoons took on wartime themes. By midyear, Donald went to an induction center in *Donald Gets Drafted*, and Pluto became *The Army Mascot*. Besides war-themed cartoons, audiences were able to take their minds off the war with such films as *Symphony Hour*, *Donald's Snow Fight*, *How to Play Baseball*, and *Pluto at the Zoo*.

Not all of the cartoon films made by Disney were made for RKO to release. There were also a number of films, produced for the government, which were meant to entertain and educate. There was *Food Will Win the War* for the Department of Agriculture, and *Out of the Frying Pan into the Firing Line*, about the importance of saving waste fats needed for the manufacture of explosives, but the most successful of these films by far was one for the Treasury Department. *The New Spirit*, rushed through the Studio in record time, went into theaters to try to persuade Americans to pay their income taxes on time as the money was so necessary for the war effort. Donald Duck was chosen to star in the film, and a vast percentage of Americans testified that it encouraged them to pay their taxes promptly. The film was

SYMPHONY HOUR

FOOD WILL WIN THE WAR

WARTIME PROPAGANDA POSTER

BAMBI AND FALINE AS ADULTS

BAMBI

WALT BROUGHT FAWNS TO THE STUDIO FOR HIS ARTISTS TO STUDY

even nominated for an Academy Award, as a documentary. These films ended up competing against Disney's regularly distributed product, with theater owners not wanting to pay for Mickey or Donald when they got the non–RKO-distributed Disney cartoons for free from the government.

The animated feature for the year was *Bambi*, and it would be the last of its kind for eight years. The war, the loss of many of the Disney animators to military service, restrictions in obtaining priority materials, and intense financial pressures brought a halt to animated feature production. For *Bambi*, the Disney artists pulled out all the stops, and their animation of the forest animals was some of the most realistic they had ever done. But while *Bambi* was well received (except perhaps by deer hunters), it initially failed to make back its cost. Walt Disney was in for some tough years economically, and his feature production would suffer as a result.

☆1943

With the war continuing to rage in both Europe and the Far East, more and more training films were requested by the Army, Navy, and other government agencies, which meant that the Disney Studio's theatrical output was sharply curtailed. Only 13 cartoons were released in 1943, a third less than in 1942, and many of them had wartime themes. If it wasn't Donald in *Fall Out—Fall In, The Old Army Game,* or *Home Defense,* it was Goofy in *Victory Vehicles* or Pluto in *Private Pluto.* The latter cartoon marked the first appearance of the pesky chipmunks who would soon be known as Chip 'n' Dale.

The Academy Award-winning cartoon was *Der Fuehrer's Face,* a strongly anti-Nazi film in which Donald Duck has a nightmare that he is living in "Nutziland" and working on a munitions assembly line. For the first year since *Steamboat Willie,* there was no Mickey Mouse cartoon (and there wouldn't be one for four more years). Donald Duck and the others had clearly taken his place.

A documentary film, *The Grain that Built a Hemisphere,* made under the auspices of the Coordinator of Inter-American Affairs, received an Academy Award nomination. Other films for the Coordinator warned against malaria-carrying mosquitoes (*The Winged Scourge*), water pollution (*Water, Friend or Enemy*), and germs (*Defense Against Invasion*). In all, the output of footage from the Disney

FALL OUT—FALL IN

WALT DISNEY'S
Pluto in
PRIVATE PLUTO
In Technicolor

Distributed by RKO RADIO Pictures, Inc.

DER FUEHRER'S FACE

Introducing JOE CARIOCA
THE BRAZILIAN JITTERBIRD

WALT DISNEY Goes South American
IN HIS GAYEST MUSICAL TECHNICOLOR FEATURE

SALUDOS AMIGOS (HELLO FRIENDS)

DISTRIBUTED BY RKO RADIO PICTURES INC.

SALUDOS AMIGOS
SKETCH BY MARY
BLAIR

VICTORY THROUGH AIR POWER

VICTORY THROUGH AIR POWER

Studio was the highest in its history, with 94 percent of it being produced for the government.

The year's feature films were both related to the war. The first, *Saludos Amigos*, which had had a premiere in Rio de Janeiro the previous August, was the first film to come out of the Disney artists' 1941 goodwill trip to Latin America. Its four cartoon segments with Latin American themes were tied together by live-action footage, some of it taken by Walt himself, of the Disney artists on their trip. Walt was extremely proud that the film received three Oscar nominations and made enough money that he did not need to ask for a promised government subsidy.

The second feature, *Victory Through Air Power,* was a strong propaganda film—combining live action with animation—that promoted Major Alexander de Seversky's idea that only long range airpower would win the war.

1944

With the wartime cutback in entertainment production at the Disney Studio, there was no theatrical feature ready for release in 1944. Instead, Walt Disney began what would eventually become a regular Disney policy—the rerelease of an earlier feature. It had been more than six years since *Snow White and the Seven Dwarfs* had premiered, and now there was a new generation of families that could enjoy it. So, in February, *Snow White* became the first Disney feature to be rereleased. With cartoon production again cut back—only 12 this year—the rerelease helped bring in some much-needed revenue, saving the day by accounting for a substantial portion of the year's income.

SNOW WHITE IS RERELEASED

It looked as if the war was starting to move in the favor of the Allies, beginning with D-Day in Europe (where "Mickey Mouse" was a code word) and increasing successes in the Pacific. With a return to peacetime was the hope of renewed financial success to the floundering Disney company.

HOW TO PLAY FOOTBALL

HOW TO BE A SAILOR

HOW TO PLAY GOLF

1944 was also the year that Goofy's "How to" series really took off, with *How to Be a Sailor, How to Play Golf*, and *How to Play Football*. The Motion Picture Academy recognized the football film with an Oscar nomination. Americans were tiring of the war, which had been upsetting their lives for too long, and the Disney cartoons mirrored that feeling. Domestic themes took over, and in only one cartoon (*Commando Duck*) was Donald still in the military.

WALT DISNEY POSES WITH A CAMERA

THE FLYING GAUCHITO FROM THE THREE CABALLEROS

THE THREE CABALLEROS—
DONALD DUCK, PANCHITO,
AND JOSÉ CARIOCA

THE COLD-BLOODED PENGUIN
FROM THE THREE CABALLEROS

WALT PROMOTES THE THREE
CABALLEROS

☆1945☞

In February of 1945, after a premiere the previous Christmas season in Mexico City, *The Three Caballeros*, the second film to come out of Walt Disney's 1941 trip to Latin America, was released in the U.S. More elaborate and a half hour longer than its predecessor, *Saludos Amigos*, this film added a Mexican charro rooster, Panchito, to the team of Donald Duck and José Carioca, and the trio became the Three Caballeros.

As the war was winding down, there was a general lessening of the need for training films by the government. The last five projects were completed for the Army, but a record ten educational films were made for Latin American countries under the contract with the Coordinator of Inter-American Affairs. These films covered such topics as *Hookworm, Insects as Carriers of Disease, Cleanliness Brings Health, Tuberculosis,* and *How Disease Travels* (including animation showing how to build a latrine).

The surrender of Germany in May and Japan in September ended WWII, and Disney held great hopes for the reopening of the foreign markets for its films. As the war veterans returned to their jobs at Disney, Walt was anxious to begin rebuilding an inventory of entertainment projects, which had been neglected during the war years. But despite a general euphoria over the return to peacetime, Walt would soon discover that it would be a major struggle to bring the Disney Studio back to its prewar footing.

Because of the difficulty in putting together the financing for another full-length animated feature (which could take three to four years to produce) Walt Disney decided on an alternative. He would have his artists work on a series of short films, which could be combined together and released as a feature package. He hoped that this would bring in more revenue than a group of short cartoons released individually, and keep the Disney name in the public eye.

The first "package" film was *Make Mine Music*, released in August of 1946, and containing such entertaining and diverse shorts as *The Martins and the Coys*, *Casey at the Bat*, *Peter and the Wolf*, *Johnny Fedora and Alice Bluebonnet*, and *The Whale Who Wanted to Sing at the Met*. Famous actors, musicians, and singers were gathered to perform for the soundtrack—including Jerry Colonna, the Andrews Sisters, Nelson Eddy, Benny Goodman, Dinah Shore, and Andy Russell.

Another way that would enable him to rush product out into theaters, Walt decided, was to start shooting live action films. A live-action film could be shot, edited, and sent out to theaters in a fraction of the time

CASEY AT THE BAT

PETER AND THE WOLF

AFTER YOU'VE GONE

necessary for an animated feature. However, since distributor RKO and theater owners felt that the public expected animation in a Disney film, Walt decided that he should combine live action and animation in his next project. The film was *Song of the South*, the warm story of a young boy, Johnny, who received sage advice from wise old Uncle Remus on his grandmother's plantation. Populating Uncle

SONG OF THE SOUTH

BRER RABBIT FROM *SONG OF THE SOUTH*

Remus's stories told to Johnny was a group of delightful animated characters—Brer Rabbit, Brer Fox, and Brer Bear. The young stars of the film, Bobby Driscoll and Luana Patten, were the first actors to be put under contract at the Disney Studio. James Baskett, who portrayed Uncle Remus with great warmth, would be presented with a special Academy Award, and the film would win for Best Song—"Zip-a-Dee-Doo-Dah."

With the ending of wartime restrictions, character merchandise licensing began to expand rapidly. Ingersoll brought back the Mickey Mouse watch in a popular new style, and it again became a best seller.

NEW STYLE OF MICKEY MOUSE WATCH

Meanwhile, Walt's attempts to rebuild his inventory of films required heavy borrowing from the bank. In order to balance rising labor costs with potential revenue, the Disney Studio had to lay off 300 workers in August. Theater audiences, who during the war had flocked to almost any films that were screened at their local theaters, became more discriminating. Revenues declined as competition among filmmakers increased.

☆1947

With cost-saving measures in place and his staff pared down, Walt Disney was pleased to see the company starting to make some money. In fact, 1947's gross income was the company's highest so far—over $6 million.

The package feature of the year was a bit different, since it only contained two parts. *Fun and Fancy Free* combined *Bongo*, the Sinclair Lewis story of a little circus bear, with *Mickey and the Beanstalk*, in which Mickey and his friends climb the beanstalk to try to outwit Willie the Giant. The latter film marked a turning point in Walt Disney's career. Until now, he had spoken for his primary character, Mickey Mouse. But, finding that more important things were keeping him busy, Walt turned the task of being Mickey's voice over to one of his sound effects men, Jim Macdonald.

MICKEY AND THE BEANSTALK FROM *FUN AND FANCY FREE*

SOUND EFFECTS MAN AND NEW VOICE OF MICKEY MOUSE JIM MACDONALD

WALT AND SHARON VISIT ALASKA

Merchandising was picking up too; Kay Kamen issued his first postwar Disney merchandise catalog. In the comic books, a character who would become one of the most popular of all time was created—Uncle Scrooge, in the Donald Duck story "Christmas on Bear Mountain." Artist Carl Barks, who had begun as a Disney storyman in the 1930s, had moved on to the comic books in 1942, where he found his niche.

☆1948☁

After a vacation trip to Alaska the previous August with his daughter Sharon, Walt became intrigued with the area. He had sent a husband-and-wife team of photographers, Al and Elma Milotte, up to the far north to film all aspects of human and animal life in the area, and he began to look at the footage they were submitting with greater interest. The travelogue aspects of the film footage did not seem to have possibilities, but another aspect did—footage of seals on the Pribilof Islands. Here, Walt felt, would be a fascinating film. The footage was edited so that all indication of man's presence was omitted, and the result was the 27-minute *Seal Island.*

Walt proudly called his film a True-Life Adventure, but he was amazed when RKO did not show the same interest in it that he did. So, in order to prove his point, he persuaded a friend who ran a theater in Pasadena to run the film for a week in order to qualify

SEAL ISLAND

for an Academy Award; sure enough, *Seal Island* was presented with an Oscar for Best Two-Reel Short Subject. This was an auspicious beginning for a series that would run for over a decade.

Another package feature made its way to movie theaters—*Melody Time*. Similar in concept and execution to *Make Mine Music, Melody Time* contained seven sequences, including *Bumble Boogie* (Freddy Martin and His Orchestra), *Johnny Appleseed* (Dennis Day), *Little Toot* (a return by the Andrews Sisters), and *Pecos Bill* (Roy Rogers and the Sons of the Pioneers). The segments of this and the other package features would see future use individually in theaters and on television and video.

JOHNNY APPLESEED SKETCH

BUMBLE BOOGIE

PECOS BILL

Studio animators also prepared a full complement of 16 short cartoons. Mickey again returned for two cartoons (*Mickey Down Under* and *Mickey and the Seal,* the latter nominated for an Academy Award). Donald also had a nominee—*Tea for Two Hundred.* Movie theaters seemed to have an increasing appetite for cartoons—many of the theaters held Saturday matinees where a string of cartoons would keep kids occupied while Mom and Dad were busy with their chores.

Realizing that the package features were only stopgap measures and that he would have to get to work on a real feature in order to turn the company around, Walt and his staff began serious production on *Cinderella.* In the annual report he noted, "Today we have back with us virtually all our top artists, and we can truly say that *Cinderella* will be our first postwar cartoon picture on a grand scale."

As his daughters were growing into their teenage years, Walt relished "Daddy's Day," the Sunday outings after church where he would take the girls to local zoos, playgrounds, and carnivals. But these jaunts often bored Walt. He would be sitting on a bench munching peanuts while they rode the merry-go-round, and had all the fun. This led him to consider an amusement park of his own, to be built on a tract of land across the street from his studio, a park where kids and their parents could have fun together. A memo outlined his ideas for "Mickey Mouse Park," which would feature a turn-of-the-century town with its town square, a Western Village, and a Carnival section. This was the germ of an idea which, while unfeasible then, would continue to intrigue him over the next few years.

TEA FOR TWO HUNDRED

The Walt Disney Studio

released two features in 1949, another combination of live action and animation starring Bobby Driscoll and Luana Patten—*So Dear to My Heart*— and the last of the animated package films—*The Adventures of Ichabod and Mr. Toad*. The former told the story of a boy who raises a rascally black lamb and plans to show him off at the county fair. The film included some short animated segments, primarily cut-outs from the boy's scrapbook that come to life. The latter featured Washington Irving's story, *The Legend of Sleepy Hollow*, told by Bing Crosby, and Kenneth Grahame's *Wind in the Willows*, told by Basil Rathbone.

Meanwhile, the world of Disney merchandising continued to expand. The five-millionth Mickey Mouse watch was sold, and licensees started gearing up for *Cinderella*. But a tragic event was to rock the Disney company— licensing manager Kay Kamen was killed in a plane crash. Roy Disney reorganized the company's merchandise licensing and decided to continue Kamen's work in-house. In addition, Roy and Walt decided to start the Walt Disney Music Company, to help them retain control of music copyrights and find additional ways to use the songs from the Disney films.

SO DEAR TO MY HEART

ICHABOD CRANE AND KATRINA FROM *THE ADVENTURES OF ICHABOD AND MR. TOAD*

J. THADDEUS TOAD FROM *THE ADVENTURES OF ICHABOD AND MR. TOAD*

WALT DISNEY SITS FOR A PORTRAIT

1950 TO 1974

"I do not make films primarily for children. I make them for the child in all of us, whether we be six or sixty."

WALT DISNEY

> "If it's an amusement park, it's the gosh-darnedest, most happily inspired, most carefully planned, most adventure-filled park ever conceived..."

CINDERELLA

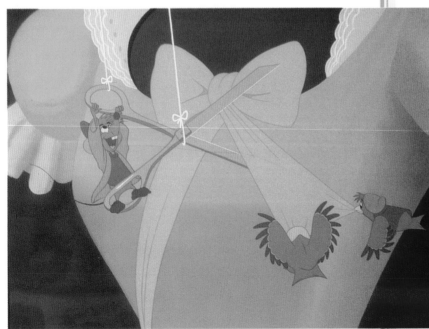

JAQ THE MOUSE FROM *CINDERELLA*

☆1950

Whatever money the Disneys could pull together had been earmarked for investing in major changes to take place this year. If the products of these changes were unsuccessful, it was very possible that the company would not survive. But Walt seemed to have a Midas touch in 1950.

Hopes were riding primarily on *Cinderella*, the elaborate animated feature that had been in production for several years. Its success was vital to ensure the continuance of animation at the Disney Studio. Labor and material costs had been growing, and Walt needed a big success to provide the confidence to continue with a regular animation program.

Cinderella provided that success. Critics raved about it, favorably comparing it to *Snow White*, and audiences flocked to the theaters to see it, making it one of the highest grossing films of the year. The film's score and the song "Bibbidi-Bobbidi-Boo" would be nominated for Oscars. The program to produce new animated features at the Disney Studio now moved full speed ahead.

Meanwhile, in order to counter the nagging problem of funds in England blocked by export regulations and at the same time get a feature film into theaters in short order, Walt determined to make a live-action historical adventure film across the Atlantic. Disney favorite Bobby Driscoll was sent to England to join a stellar British cast, which included Robert Newton, Basil Sydney, and Finlay Currie, in Robert Louis Stevenson's *Treasure Island*. The film, Walt Disney's first completely live-action feature, was released in the summer to wide acclaim.

On the same bill with *Treasure Island* was the second of the True-Life Adventure featurettes, *Beaver Valley*. Following in the footsteps of its predecessor, it also would win an Oscar. Among the other shorts released, Donald's *Crazy Over Daisy* became a classic, and Goofy's *Motor Mania* would go on to be utilized for driver training classes for decades to come.

Another medium that interested the Disney brothers was television. While Walt and Roy Disney had been closely watching the growth of this new medium, they had held off on pursuing any projects until they could be assured of success. The opportunity came when Coca-Cola desired a special for airing on Christmas afternoon. Disney pulled out all the stops to produce a classy product. Walt himself appeared as host on the hour-long show, which he used to promote his upcoming feature, *Alice in Wonderland*. This initial plunge

WALT SURVEYS THE SET
FOR HIS FIRST
TELEVISION SPECIAL

into television was hailed by critics as an entertainment and production triumph. The show was seen by an estimated 20 million viewers, at a time when there were only 10.5 million television sets in the whole country.

Disney had now reached the middle of the century, and the bottom line could not have looked better, showing a profit after two years of losses. The two features did well, and character merchandising revenues were up 50 percent for the first year that the licensing was handled by a direct operating division of the company.

The only feature-length motion picture released in 1951 was the animated feature *Alice in Wonderland*. Walt Disney did his best to transform this highly regarded yet bizarre tale into an animated movie, but in the end he would later claim that *Alice* had no "heart." Perhaps this was the reason for its lack of commercial success.

Released with *Alice in Wonderland* was the True-Life Adventure featurette *Nature's Half Acre*. Telling the story of the amazing variety of life

ALICE IN WONDERLAND CEL

found during each season in almost any plot of land, the film garnered an Oscar for Best Two-Reel Short Subject.

1951 also brought with it the last Pluto cartoon, *Cold Turkey*. Goofy, on the other hand, had a banner year with his series of shorts—more cartoons than in any other year. His record seven cartoons included *Lion Down*, *Home Made Home* and *Fathers Are People*.

This year also saw another Disney television program. Shortly after he turned 50, Walt produced his second television special, the *Walt Disney Christmas Show*, which aired on Christmas Day. The program was essentially a tool used to promote his upcoming animated feature, *Peter Pan*.

ANIMATOR WARD KIMBALL DRAWS THE MAD HATTER FOR *ALICE IN WONDERLAND* AS WALT WATCHES

FATHERS ARE PEOPLE

✯1952

On March 27, 1952, the headline of the *Burbank Daily Review* read: WALT DISNEY MAKE-BELIEVE LAND PROJECT PLANNED HERE. Expanding upon his earlier ideas for a Mickey Mouse Park, Walt had moved forward

COLD TURKEY

with his plans for the project, now to be called Disneyland, and he was considering as the site a 16-acre plot on Riverside Drive in Burbank, directly across the street from the Disney Studio. However, Walt quickly realized the dreams he had for Disneyland had rapidly outgrown this little parcel of land, so the search was on for a new Southern California site.

In the meantime, Walt began to assemble a team of the Studio's most talented and inventive staff members to start working on the Disneyland project. The members of this creative team were the first to join the newly formed WED Enterprises. This design and development organization, founded by Walt in December, occupied a portion of the Burbank studio lot and was the precursor of today's Walt Disney Imagineering. With the formation of WED Enterprises, it was now official: the creative design process for Disneyland was underway.

In 1952, the Studio again released only one new feature film into theaters—the live-action adventure *The Story of Robin Hood and His Merrie Men*, with Richard Todd as the infamous outlaw.

A host of popular animated shorts were also produced by the Studio this year. Among the 17 cartoons was *Lambert, the Sheepish Lion*, which was nominated for an Academy Award. Battle ensued when Chip and Dale took over one of Donald Duck's apple trees in *Donald Applecore*, and in *Trick or Treat*, Donald tormented Huey, Dewey and Louie on Halloween but eventually got his when Witch Hazel joined up with the three nephews to teach him a lesson.

LAMBERT, THE SHEEPISH LION

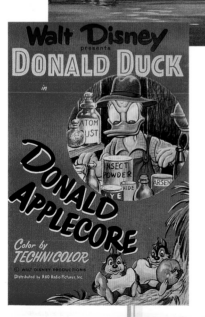

TRICK OR TREAT

AMOS MOUSE FROM *BEN AND ME*

⭐1953

Many of the Studio's 1953 releases went on to be Academy Award-winning or nominated films. Walt Disney's first feature-length True-Life Adventure film, *The Living Desert*, which showed the breadth of life in a region of arid desolation, won the Oscar for Best Documentary. The first of 17 People and Places travelogue featurettes, *The Alaskan Eskimo*, would win an Academy Award for Best Documentary Short Subject, and the True-Life Adventure featurette, *Bear Country*, would win for Best Two-Reel Short Subject. The fourth 1953 Disney production to garner an Oscar was *Toot, Whistle, Plunk and Boom*, in which Professor Owl explains the history of musical instruments from the age of cave dwellers to modern times. Academy Award nominees included *Ben and Me* and *Rugged Bear*.

DONALD DUCK IN *RUGGED BEAR*

Peter Pan, the tremendously popular play by Sir James M. Barrie, was released as Disney's latest animated feature. The story of the magical boy who wouldn't grow up, *Peter Pan* became an instant classic.

PETER, TINKER BELL, AND THE DARLING CHILDREN IN *PETER PAN*

(AT LEFT) PETER, WENDY AND TINKER BELL IN *PETER PAN;* (AT RIGHT) CAPTAIN HOOK, MR. SMEE AND THE CROCODILE

Other releases of 1953 included the swashbuckling live-action feature *The Sword and the Rose*, starring Richard Todd and Glynis Johns. The cartoon *Adventures in Music: Melody* featured Professor Owl teaching his class about melody. It was the first cartoon ever to be filmed in 3-D. Also of note was the Mickey Mouse short *The Simple Things*. This would be the last cartoon to star the famous mouse for 30 years.

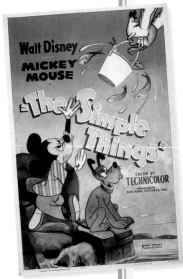

Though animation was going strong, distributor RKO felt the feature-length True-Life Adventure films that Walt was producing would fail. Walt disagreed and knew the films would be popular with audiences. This discrepancy provoked Walt and Roy Disney to break away from RKO, the company that had distributed the Studio's films to theaters since 1937, and to form their own motion picture distribution organization, Buena Vista Distribution Company. RKO lost the contract to distribute Disney's

films, and *The Living Desert* became the first release handled by Buena Vista Distribution. Walt was right—*The Living Desert* earned $5 million during its original release and cost only $500,000 to produce.

In July of this year, Walt hired the Stanford Research Institute to scout a Southern California location that would be suitable for Disneyland. By August the site had been found—38 miles south of Burbank in a city called Anaheim. The time had also come to pitch prospective backers on the idea of Disneyland in order to secure funding for the project. Since network executives had approached him in the past about doing a television series, Walt felt that his greatest hope for funding lay within the television industry. But when he tied Disneyland to his proposed television series, he was turned down by both NBC and CBS. Roy then scheduled a meeting with executives at ABC, a fledgling network that was desperate for quality programming.

On a September Saturday, Walt had tracked down Herb Ryman, an artist friend, to help him draw a detailed rendering of what Disneyland would look like. Over the weekend, which came to be known as the "lost weekend," Walt talked about his vision for Disneyland while Herb drew. Roy took the detailed drawing with him and it managed to turn the tide. ABC agreed to loan Disney $500,000 and guarantee $4.5 million in loans in return for a one-third ownership in Disneyland and a promise of a weekly Disney television show for the network.

☆1954

In April of 1954, just 90 days before construction was to begin on Disneyland, Walt brought retired Admiral Joe Fowler on board to supervise the project. To Fowler, Disneyland looked like a lot of what he called "blue sky plans," but the man known as "Admiral Can-Do," who once ran the busy San Francisco Navy Yard, was perfect for the job. As the months passed, tropical jungles, a rustic frontier fort and a charming, ornate castle started to take the place of what was once Anaheim orange groves.

As construction began on Disneyland the theme park, on October 27, *Disneyland* the television series debuted on ABC. Each week, the show was hosted by Walt and featured programs from the realms of Fantasyland, Adventureland, Frontierland and Tomorrowland. Viewers were also treated to frequent "Progress Reports," in which actual Disneyland construction footage was shown to pique the interest of would-be guests. ABC was thrilled with the program's tremendously high ratings and the Emmy it won as Best Variety Series during its first season.

As part of the *Disneyland* show, the first episode of the wildly popular *Davy Crockett* mini-series, *Davy Crockett—Indian Fighter*, aired with

WALT AND ADM. JOE FOWLER CHECK OUT DISNEYLAND CONSTRUCTION

WALT DESCRIBING DISNEYLAND TO HIS TELEVISION AUDIENCE

Fess Parker starring in the role that would make him famous. A Davy Crockett craze instantly spread across America, starting a run on coonskin caps. "The Ballad of Davy Crockett" soared to the top of the Hit Parade, where it remained for a whopping 16 weeks. Nationwide, Disney's licensees ultimately sold more than $300 million worth of Davy Crockett merchandise. *Davy Crockett* had carved its niche as a part of Americana and was a television phenomenon that would remain unsurpassed for years to come.

Meanwhile, the Studio released three feature films, the first being *Rob Roy, the Highland Rogue*, star-ring Richard Todd in his third and final role at Disney. The second True-Life Adventure feature, *The Vanishing Prairie*, was released, and would win an Academy Award. The film also caused some surprising controversy when the New York State Censorship Board banned it over a scene showing the birth of a baby buffalo. Walt Disney, whose name was synonymous with the finest in family entertainment, had been censored. Walt was quoted as saying, "It would be a shame if New York children had to believe the stork brings buffaloes, too." The censors eventually reversed the decision, and the film was shown in its entirety.

Based on the classic story by Jules Verne, the action-adventure film *20,000 Leagues Under the Sea* opened to eager audiences. The highly successful film starred James Mason, Kirk Douglas, Paul Lukas and Peter Lorre, and featured the popular song "A Whale of a Tale," sung by Douglas. It was also the first Disney feature filmed in CinemaScope. *20,000 Leagues* won Academy Awards for Best Special Effects and Best Art Direction/Set Decoration, and was nominated for Best Film Editing.

(ABOVE) A GIANT SQUID ATTACKS IN *20,000 LEAGUES UNDER THE SEA;* (AT RIGHT) THE *NAUTILUS*

WALT TOOK HOME FOUR OSCARS IN 1954

Operation Undersea, a television show hosted by Walt Disney, detailed the history of sea exploration, then took viewers for a behind-the-scenes look at the making of *20,000 Leagues Under the Sea*, demonstrating new techniques invented for underwater filming. For all intents and purposes, the show was a one-hour commercial for the new Disney movie, but it was so well produced that it won the Emmy for Best Individual Show of the year.

In the Disney family, Walt's daughter Diane married Ron Miller, and Roy E. Disney, Roy's son, began working at the Studio as an assistant film editor on the True-Life Adventure films.

☆1955

After one full year of rigorous construction demands and a total investment of $17 million, the gates of Disneyland opened for its first guests on Sunday, July 17, 1955. On day one, the Park offered five themed "lands"—Adventureland, Frontierland, Fantasyland, Tomorrowland and Main Street, U.S.A.—with a total of 20 attractions.

Charming turn-of-the-century Main Street featured quaint Victorian architecture, the Horse-Drawn Street Cars, the Disneyland Railroad and a host of shops and restaurants recalling a bygone era. In Adventureland, the Jungle Cruise took guests on a safari adventure along the lush, winding tropical rivers of the world, while Frontierland boasted an authentic-looking wilderness fort, the grand Mark Twain Riverboat and the Golden Horseshoe Revue. Upon crossing the drawbridge of Sleeping Beauty Castle, guests entered Fantasyland, the home

DISNEYLAND TICKET #1

THE FIRST PAYING GUESTS TO DISNEYLAND—MICHAEL SCHWARTNER AND CHRISTINE VESS

TWA ROCKETSHIP READY FOR RAISING

of Walt Disney's most beloved animated characters. Among Tomorrowland's offerings were Space Station X-1, Rocket to the Moon, Monsanto Hall of Chemistry, Aluminum Hall of Fame and a popular *20,000 Leagues Under the Sea* exhibit.

The highly anticipated Opening Day festivities were covered by ABC with a 90-minute live special, *Dateline Disneyland*, hosted by television personalities Art Linkletter, Ronald Reagan and Bob Cummings.

Disneyland opened to rave reviews. The *Minneapolis Tribune*'s Will Jones wrote, "If it's an amusement park, it's the gosh-darnedest, most happily

MAIN STREET U.S.A. CONSTRUCTION

VICTORIAN ARCHITECTURE ON ONE SIDE, JUNGLE ARCHITECTURE ON THE OTHER

SLEEPING BEAUTY CASTLE CONSTRUCTION

REHEARSAL FOR OPENING DAY DEDICATION CEREMONY

(CLOCKWISE FROM TOP) CLOCK OF THE WORLD AT THE ENTRANCE TO TOMORROWLAND; JUNGLE CRUISE IN ADVENTURELAND; FRONTIERLAND; GOLDEN HORSESHOE REVUE IN FRONTIERLAND; SLEEPING BEAUTY CASTLE

inspired, most carefully planned, most adventure-filled park ever conceived. No ride or concession in it is like anything in any other amusement park anywhere."

Walt's dream for Disneyland had finally become a reality. The fruits of his labor, and the labor of his team of designers, resulted in a magical land that would become a veritable vacation mecca for families all around the world. In fact, on September 8, only seven weeks after the opening of Disneyland, Elsa Marquez was welcomed as the Park's one-millionth guest—Disneyland was a hit!

TOWN SQUARE

WALT WITH CALIFORNIA GOVERNOR KNIGHT AND FRED GURLEY, PRESIDENT OF THE SANTA FE RAILROAD

WALT EXPLAINED THE HISTORY OF ANIMATION ON TELEVISION IN *THE STORY OF THE ANIMATED DRAWING*

LADY AND THE TRAMP

In addition to the success of Disneyland, the *Mickey Mouse Club*, one of the most popular children's television programs of all time, made its ABC debut on October 3. The hour-long show starred 24 talented kids known as Mouseketeers, who performed skits, musical numbers and introduced special guest stars, serials and Disney cartoons. Many of the Mouseketeers, including Annette, Tommy, Darlene, Lonnie, Sharon, Sherry, Doreen, Bobby, Cubby, Karen, Dennis, Cheryl and their adult leaders Jimmie Dodd and Roy Williams, became instant celebrities.

Meanwhile, on the big screen, *Lady and the Tramp*, the delightful tale of two dogs from different worlds, was the Studio's latest animated feature release. The idea for the film came from a short story, *Happy Dan, the Whistling Dog,* by Ward Greene. It was the first Cinema-Scope animated feature and included the popular songs "He's a Tramp" and "The Siamese Cat Song," both of which were co-written and sung by Peggy Lee.

Man *in Space* aired on television, with several noted space scientists explaining the challenges of space exploration, including what they perceived to be the problems of weightlessness. The People and Places featurette *Men Against the Arctic* showed how an ice-breaker, a specially constructed U.S. Coast Guard ship, maneuvers through heavy Arctic icepack. The film would win the Academy Award for Best Documentary Short Subject.

FANTASY IN THE SKY FIREWORKS OVER
SLEEPING BEAUTY CASTLE

✩1956☁

In its second year of operation, Disneyland saw the opening of more than a dozen new attractions—the most to be added in a single year in the Park's entire history. Among them were the Junior Autopia, Astro Jets, Tom Sawyer Island, Rainbow Caverns Mine Train and Storybook Land.

By October, Disneyland had welcomed five million guests, including visitors from every state in the United States and over 60 foreign countries. The Park also introduced its spectacular Fantasy in the Sky fireworks display, which has since become a perennial favorite during the summer season.

Actor Fess Parker had a busy year at the Disney Studios, starring in three of the year's four new movies. The first film released was *The Great Locomotive Chase.* Based on a true incident during the Civil War, Parker played James J. Andrews, a daring Union spy who, along with his men,

stole a train from under the noses of four thousand Confederate troops. Two Davy Crockett episodes from the *Disneyland* television series were released theatrically as *Davy Crockett and the River Pirates*, with Parker in the title role. *Westward Ho the Wagons!* featured Parker as a wagon train leader on a trek through the unexplored terrain of America's new frontier.

TOM SAWYER ISLAND AND STORYBOOK LAND CANAL BOATS WERE ADDED IN 1956

THE GREAT LOCOMOTIVE CHASE

1957

The Walt Disney Studio released three feature films in 1957, starting with the American Revolution-themed *Johnny Tremain*. Hal Stalmaster played the title character, a patriotic young man who risked all

OLD YELLER

to do his part in the colonists' struggle for independence from the British. *Old Yeller*, the classic tale of a boy and his dog, became one of the most beloved Disney films of all time. The movie, which starred Dorothy McGuire, Fess Parker, Tommy Kirk and Kevin Corcoran, tells of a faithful yellow dog who proves his unwavering loyalty to the Coates family by saving Arliss from a bear, Mrs. Coates from a wolf and Travis from wild pigs. Despite his bravery, Yeller contracts rabies, and in one of the most memorable

PERRI

scenes in motion picture history, young Travis must shoot his canine companion. Disney's first and only True-Life Fantasy, *Perri*, chronicled the life of a little pine squirrel. The Academy Award-nominated film was based on a story by Felix Salten, who had also written the original story for what became Walt Disney's masterpiece, *Bambi*.

The Wetback Hound, a live-action featurette about a

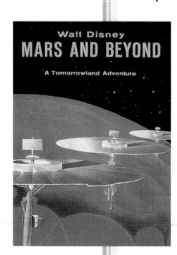

young dog named Paco who is mistreated by his owners in Mexico and travels to the United States in search of a kindly master, won, among other awards, the Academy Award for Best Live-Action Short Subject.

On television, Disney introduced a new hero to audiences with Zorro, the bold renegade who defended the poor from the tyranny of oppressive military forces. This masked avenger, whose alter ego was the mild-mannered Don Diego de la Vega, was played in dashing style by Guy Williams. A total of 78 half-hour *Zorro* episodes were produced during the show's two-year run.

For the *Disneyland* television series, legendary Disney animator Ward Kimball directed the animated show *Mars and Beyond*, which gave viewers a humorous look at what humans might discover on Mars, in addition to predictions about exploration of the planet. The *Mickey Mouse Club* began its third season, continuing to dominate the daytime national audience ratings.

Several new attractions were added to Disneyland Park in 1957. In Tomorrowland, the Viewliner, a precursor to the Monorail, began operating, and the Monsanto House of the Future, a modernistic, four-winged house built

WALT DISNEY STUDIOS present ZORRO

of plastic, welcomed its first visitors. Shirley Temple was on hand to help dedicate a new attraction inside Sleeping Beauty Castle, where one could observe meticulously crafted dioramas from the upcoming animated feature. A new tradition started this year with the first annual New Year's Eve Party, which remains a popular celebration today.

☆ 1958 ☁

In its fifth season, the Disney television anthology series changed its name to *Walt Disney Presents*, and two more television heroes, Elfego Baca and Texas John Slaughter, were introduced. *The Nine Lives of Elfego*

Baca was a ten-part series about an Old West gunman who becomes a lawyer to defend the oppressed and falsely accused. *Texas John Slaughter* followed the adventures of a Texas Ranger who fights bandits, outlaws, cattle rustlers and other shady characters.

Also in 1958, three feature films were released by the Studio. For the Academy Award-winning True-Life Adventure *White Wilderness*, the film crew spent three years in the frigid Arctic regions of Canada and Alaska, filming polar bears, gray wolves, caribou, reindeer, walrus, ring seals, white Beluga whales and other animals in their natural habitats. *The Light in the Forest* was a tale about the struggles faced by a young man who is raised as an

(CLOCKWISE FROM LEFT) MONSANTO HOUSE OF THE FUTURE IN TOMORROWLAND; SLEEPING BEAUTY CASTLE DIORAMA; DISNEYLAND'S FIRST NEW YEAR'S EVE PARTY TICKET; WALT DISNEY ON THE MARK TWAIN RIVERBOAT WITH ADMIRAL JOE FOWLER

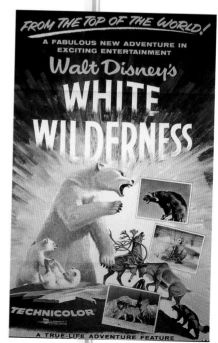

SAILING SHIP COLUMBIA

GRAND CANYON DIORAMA

Indian and then forced to return to his white family, and *Tonka* followed the adventures of a young Indian brave named White Bull and his stallion, which he names Tonka Wakan, meaning The Great One. Tonka became the sole cavalry survivor of the Battle of the Little Big Horn.

At Disneyland Park, the Sailing Ship Columbia, modeled after the first vessel to successfully circumnavigate the globe, took its maiden voyage around the Rivers of America in Frontierland. Guests aboard the Disneyland Railroad were treated to the new Grand Canyon Diorama, and in Fantasyland, a new ride, Alice in Wonderland, based on the fanciful animated feature, also opened.

Another debut was the first Candlelight Procession which took place at Disneyland during the 1958 Christmas season. The ceremony would become a long-standing Christmastime tradition, hosted each year by a celebrity narrator telling the Christmas story as massed choirs sing favorite carols.

QUEEN OF HEARTS IN ALICE IN WONDERLAND ATTRACTION

CANDLELIGHT CEREMONY

☆1959

In 1959, Walt Disney presented what was his most lavish and costly animated feature to date, *Sleeping Beauty*. The film's budget exceeded $6 million, but unfortunately *Sleeping Beauty* did not prove to be a tremendous box office success in its initial release.

(TOP) BRIAR ROSE FROM *SLEEPING BEAUTY*; (BELOW) MALEFICENT

THE SHAGGY DOG

The first Disney live-action comedy, *The Shaggy Dog*, also premiered in 1959. In the film, young Wilby Daniels inadvertently discovers a cursed ring that, after he reads its Latin inscription, turns him into a large Bratislavian sheepdog. Originally, Walt had intended for the film to be a television show, but its prospects looked good enough to merit a theatrical release. Walt's instincts were right. It turned out to be a big hit for the Studio.

JANET MUNRO AND JAMES MACARTHUR IN *THIRD MAN ON THE MOUNTAIN*

DONALD IN MATHMAGIC LAND

E TICKET

NOAH'S ARK

WALT AND
LILLY DISNEY
GREET KING
BAUDOUIN OF
BELGIUM AT
DISNEYLAND

Also released was another popular live-action Disney classic, *Darby O'Gill and the Little People*, the tale of an elderly Irishman who captures his friendly adversary, King Brian, the king of the leprechauns, who must grant Darby three wishes.

Yet another release was *Third Man on the Mountain*, the story of a young, inexperienced climber who conquers the majestic yet treacherous Citadel. The CinemaScope featurette *Grand Canyon* won the Academy Award for Best Live-Action Short Subject, and Academy Award nominations were garnered for *Donald in Mathmagic Land, Noah's Ark* and *Mysteries of the Deep.*

At Disneyland, the famous E ticket was first offered this year. It quickly earned its place as an American slang phrase, representing the ultimate thrill. In fact, astronaut Sally Ride would later call her first journey into space a "real E ticket ride." In the booklets of ride coupons, the A tickets were for the tamest rides, while the E tickets were reserved for the most elaborate and exciting ones. One of the first E ticket attractions, which opened in the summer, was the Matterhorn Bobsleds, a high-speed thrill ride on which guests careened through the caverns of a 1/100th-scale reproduction of the famous mountain.

The country's first daily operating monorail system opened in Tomorrowland. Beneath the Monorail station was the Submarine Voyage attraction, which had opened only a few days earlier and was billed as a voyage through "liquid space."

The company purchased a 708-acre ranch about 25 miles north of the Burbank studio to serve as a film location. Named the Golden Oak Ranch, the facility would be used to film future movies for Disney and other studios.

In the world of finance, the company's profits dipped slightly for the first time since 1950 due to higher production costs and a smaller margin of profit from *Sleeping Beauty*. However, the weak box office returns

on *Sleeping Beauty* were more than made up for by *The Shaggy Dog*, which became the company's highest-grossing picture. And, now that Disneyland was running smoothly, Walt quietly hired Economics Research Associates to prepare "A Study of the Market for an Eastern Disneyland."

On May 10, 1959, Walt Disney's daughter Sharon married Robert B. Brown at the Presbyterian Church in Pacific Palisades, California, with a reception immediately following at the Hotel Bel Air in Beverly Hills.

GOLDEN OAK RANCH

(AT LEFT) VICE PRESIDENT NIXON AND FAMILY HELP WALT DEDICATE THE MONORAIL

MONORAIL

☆1960

With seven new movies in theaters, Disney released more films in 1960 than in any previous year. The first release was *Toby Tyler, or Ten Weeks with a Circus*, in which Kevin Corcoran played Toby, an orphan who runs away to join a circus and becomes best friends with a chimp named Mr. Stubbs. In *Kidnapped*, young David Balfour attempts to regain his rightful inheritance, but is nearly killed, then kidnapped by his scheming Uncle Ebenezer. Several episodes of the *Zorro* series were compiled and released theatrically as *The Sign of Zorro*, and *Ten Who Dared* told the historic tale of the

struggles and dangers encountered by the men who made the perilous journey through the Grand Canyon on the Colorado River. The True-Life Adventure film series concluded with *Jungle Cat*, the story of the South American jaguar.

Walt Disney's British actress discovery Hayley Mills played her first of six roles in Disney feature films as a precocious young orphan in the classic motion picture *Pollyanna.* Another film that would earn the title of Disney classic was *Swiss Family Robinson*, which was based on the book by Johann Wyss. Because the movie was filmed on location in the Caribbean over a 22-week period, production costs quickly escalated, resulting in an astronomical $4 million budget. However, the film's extraordinary box office performance, subsequent theatrical reissues and home video releases would make it one of Disney's top-grossing film properties.

When the International Olympic Committee decided to hold its Winter

WALT AND LILLY AT THE OLYMPICS

88

Olympics in Squaw Valley, California, Walt Disney was selected to be in charge of the pageantry. Walt and his committee not only arranged the opening and closing ceremonies, but designed huge ice sculptures of athletes and other decorations for the event.

SQUAW VALLEY OLYMPICS

1961

101 Dalmatians was a phenomenal success with movie audiences. Based on the book by Dodie Smith, the film was the first animated feature to make extensive use of the Xerox process for transferring the animators' drawings to cels, the sheets of celluloid on which the characters are painted.

In addition to the animated *101 Dalmatians,* five new Disney live-action films were in the theaters. *The Absent-Minded Professor,* introduced the world to that sensational substance

(TOP) PONGO WITH PUPS IN *101 DALMATIANS*; (BELOW) *101 DALMATIANS*

101 DALMATIANS

HAYLEY MILLS WITH HAYLEY MILLS IN *THE PARENT TRAP*

FLYING SAUCERS IN
TOMORROWLAND

"flubber" (flying rubber). After winning an honorary Academy Award for most outstanding juvenile performance for *Pollyanna*, Hayley Mills starred in her second Disney role in *The Parent Trap*. Hayley did double duty for this film, playing both Sharon and Susan, twins who were separated as children but are reunited by fate at a summer camp.

Just in time for the Christmas season, the Studio released *Babes in Toyland*, a fanciful journey from Mother Goose Village to the dreaded Forest of No Return, and subsequently the wondrous Toyland. The lively musical starred Tommy Sands and Annette Funicello.

Opening at Disneyland Park this year was the Flying Saucers attraction in Tomorrowland. The attraction, which had individually operated saucers that floated over a cushion of air, was not technologically perfected and was constantly breaking down. After several years, Disneyland maintenance crews would finally give up trying to make the attraction work and it would close.

Elsewhere at Disneyland, the Monorail track was expanded, connecting the Park to the Disneyland Hotel, and Tinker Bell began her summer flights high above Fantasyland, igniting the Fantasy in the Sky fireworks. The first Disneyland Grad Nite Party, which at the time was the largest high school graduation party ever thrown in the United States, was also held.

Walt Disney's Wonderful World of Color became the new title for the Disney anthology series, and it moved from ABC to NBC. One of the main reasons Walt made the move was that NBC, unlike its rival, was willing to broadcast the Disney show in color. On the first installment of the show, Walt and his new animated character, a relative of Donald Duck named Ludwig Von Drake, demonstrated the advantage and appeal of watching Disney programs in color. Walt's amazing kaleidoscope of color prompted a rush on stores selling color television sets. Not coincidentally, RCA Victor, owner of NBC and one of the leading manufacturers of color televisions, was one of the show's sponsors.

The cartoon featurette *Donald and the Wheel* debuted, and Donald also starred in *The Litterbug*. The Goofy cartoon, *Aquamania*, was nominated for an Academy Award.

At the end of the year, Walt Disney celebrated his 60th birthday, but there seemed to be no slowdown in his creative efforts.

FIRST DISNEYLAND GRAD NITE PARTY

(FROM LEFT) GOOFY IN
AQUAMANIA; *DONALD
AND THE WHEEL*;
THE LITTERBUG

SWISS FAMILY
TREE HOUSE IN
ADVENTURELAND

TAHITIAN TERRACE IN
ADVENTURELAND

LUDWIG VON
DRAKE IN *A
SYMPOSIUM
ON POPULAR
SONGS*

CELEBRITY SPORTS
CENTER IN DENVER

There was a great deal of activity in Adventureland at Disneyland Park during 1962. The Swiss Family Tree House, which was based on Disney's popular 1960 live-action adventure film, opened. New scenes were added to the Jungle Cruise, including the ever-popular elephant bathing pool. Also opening in Adventureland was the Tahitian Terrace, a Poly-nesian-themed restaurant that included dinner and a show.

Six more live-action films were released by the Studio—*Moon Pilot, Bon Voyage, Big Red, Almost Angels, The Legend of Lobo* and *In Search of the Castaways.* In *Bon Voyage,* Fred MacMurray plays Harry Willard, a man who, after 20 years of marriage, makes good on his promise to take his wife to Europe. The film was shot on loca-tion in Europe and was nominated for Academy Awards for Best Costume Design and Best Sound. Adapted from a story by Jules Verne, *In Search of the Castaways,* starring Hayley Mills and Maurice Chevalier, chronicles the high-seas adventures of a rescue party looking for the missing captain of the S. S. *Britannia.*

The befuddled professor Ludwig Von Drake, who had been created for *Walt Disney's Wonderful World of Color* the previous year, hosted *A Symposium on Popular Songs,* a cartoon featurette about popular music. It was nomi-nated for an Academy Award.

Walt Disney Productions acquired the stock of Celebrity Sports Center in

Denver, Colorado, which had been built by a coalition of Hollywood personalities, including Walt Disney. The recreation center represented a diversification in the company's amusement and recreational business, and would in future years act as a training center for personnel expected to perform similar duties at an as of yet unplanned Florida resort.

☆1963

Son of Flubber, a sequel to the 1961 hit comedy *The Absent-Minded Professor,* was released, continuing the laboratory antics of Professor Brainard with his newest creation—a flubber hybrid called "Flubbergas." *Miracle of the White Stallions* was the story of the director of a prestigious Vienna riding school who saves the school and its majestic Lipizzan white horses in the wake of World War II, and *Savage Sam* was a sequel to the classic Disney film *Old Yeller.*

MIRACLE OF THE WHITE STALLIONS

Hayley Mills starred in one of the earliest Disney musicals, *Summer Magic,* which was based on the Kate Douglas Wiggins novel, *Mother Carey's Chickens.* In *The Incredible Journey,* three amazing animals, two dogs and a cat, embark on a 200-mile trek across the Canadian wilderness, while *The Three Lives of Thomasina* tells the tale of a girl's love for her large ginger cat, Thomasina. On Christmas Day, Disney released its newest animated feature production, *The Sword in the Stone.*

WALT DISNEY PROMOTES *THE SWORD IN THE STONE*

(TOP) A SPELL IS CAST ON ARTHUR IN *THE SWORD IN THE STONE;* (BELOW) ARTHUR AND MERLIN

93

Disneyland opened the Enchanted Tiki Room attraction in Adventureland, its first attraction to utilize the sophisticated technology of *Audio-Animatronics*® figures created by Walt Disney's team of Imagineers. The opening of the Enchanted Tiki Room brought with it the dawn of a new era in theme park entertainment—an era where amazingly lifelike robots would entertain and captivate the multitudes through the new medium of 3-D animation.

Walt Disney himself was continuing to think about the possibilities of an Eastern Disneyland. After dismissing thoughts of St. Louis and the Miami area, in November he secretly flew over areas of Central Florida in the corporate plane, looking at possible sites. He also retained attorneys to quietly search for available land.

☆1964

Walt Disney's most supercalifragilisticexpialidocious film of all, *Mary Poppins*, was released into theaters in 1964. Perhaps one of the best-known and beloved Disney films of all time, *Mary Poppins* starred Julie Andrews in one of the most outstanding performances of her career. The film was both a critical and commercial success, and a masterpiece that would remain a timeless treasure for

JANE DARWELL AS
THE BIRD WOMAN
IN *MARY POPPINS*

DAVID TOMLINSON, MATTHEW GARBER AND
KAREN DOTRICE IN *MARY POPPINS*

generations to come. Richard and Robert Sherman penned a lavish musical score and a slate of songs that instantly became some of the most popular in Disney history, including "A Spoonful of Sugar," "Feed the Birds," "Supercalifragilisticexpialidocious" and many others. *Mary Poppins* earned an incredible 13 nominations from the Academy of Motion Pictures Arts and Sciences, winning 5 Oscars, including Best Actress (Julie Andrews), Best Song ("Chim Chim Cher-ee"), Best Music Score, Best Film Editing and Best Special Visual Effects.

Other films released by the Studio in 1964 included another Hayley Mills film, *The Moon-Spinners*, *The Misadventures of Merlin Jones*, *Emil and the Detectives* and *A Tiger Walks*.

When the New York World's Fair opened its two-year exhibition, it included four attractions developed by Disney. The most well-known of the Disney contributions was It's a Small World, presented by Pepsi-Cola and UNICEF. The attraction featured hundreds of *Audio-Animatronics* children from over 100 regions of the world singing the song

"It's a Small World," which was written by the Academy Award-winning Sherman Brothers. The song is probably one of the best-known Disney tunes of all time.

For General Electric's Progressland at the fair, Disney created the Carousel of Progress, which told of the increased importance of electricity in the home, as seen through the eyes of a typical *Audio-Animatronics* American family. The attraction was housed in a large theater, in which the audience rotated around stationary stages. As part of the State of Illinois presentation at the World's Fair, Disney created his third *Audio-Animatronics* show, Great Moments with Mr. Lincoln, during which Lincoln recited excerpts from some of his most well-known speeches. The fourth attraction produced by Disney

(AT LEFT) HAYLEY MILLS IN *THE MOON-SPINNERS;* (AT RIGHT) TOMMY KIRK AND ANNETTE FUNICELLO IN *THE MISADVENTURES OF MERLIN JONES*

WALT OVERSEES PLACEMENT OF NEW ANIMALS IN THE JUNGLE CRUISE AT DISNEYLAND

for the fair was Ford's Magic Skyway, in which visitors rode in Ford cars through a world of dinosaurs and cavemen, with narration by Walt Disney himself.

The work Walt Disney did for the World's Fair was of tremendous use to him to further his plans for a second Disneyland park. Even though he had been narrowing in on Central Florida as a possible location, he was cautious, and wondered if people on the East Coast would be receptive to Disney–style attractions. He felt some research was in order, and the New York World's Fair proved to be the perfect test site. Best of all, the organizations that sponsored the fair attractions helped pay for this

research and allowed Walt to do extensive experimentation in *Audio-Animatronics*, especially on his first human characters. It came as no surprise that the longest lines at the fair were for the four attractions created by Disney. Walt's experiment was a huge success. It was clear that Disney attractions would be as popular on the East Coast as they were in Southern California. When the fair closed in 1965, Walt packed up all his attractions and used them to create new shows at Disneyland, but the positive response at the fair meant that work would soon begin on an East Coast Disney theme park.

Disneyland celebrated its

10th year with a "Tencennial" parade, and on January 3, 1965, the anniversary was celebrated on *Walt Disney's Wonderful World of Color*, with Walt introducing some of the Park's newest attractions. Julie Reihm became the Park's first "Disneyland Ambassador to the World." Also at Disneyland, the popular New York World's Fair

DISNEYLAND 10TH ANNIVERSARY CAKE

attraction, Great Moments with Mr. Lincoln, was installed in the Opera House on Main Street and today is one of the few attractions unique to Disneyland.

Perhaps the most noteworthy series of events in 1965 surrounded the top-secret project for an East Coast Disneyland, which had been given several code names at the Disney Studio, such as Project Winter and Project X. Walt and Roy had settled on Florida for their site, primarily because of climate, land cost and accessibility, and had been secretly purchasing large parcels of land in the central part of the state, near Orlando. Having learned his lesson from the cheap motels, fast-food restaurants and general urban clutter sprouting up around Disneyland, Walt was determined to buy enough land to insulate his new development from the "outside world." After all the land was acquired, Walt and Roy ended up with a whopping 27,443 acres— a parcel twice the size of Manhattan Island—which cost them approximately $5 million.

Before long, people were wondering what mysterious company was accumulating these enormous masses of land. Some believed the buyer to be Lockheed, Howard Hughes, Ford or Chrysler. On May 4, the *Orlando Sentinel* reported rumors of an "East Coast Disneyland," but it wasn't until October 25, 1965 that Florida Governor Haydon Burns confirmed the reports. Disney quickly put together a press conference in Orlando on November 15. At the conference, Walt and Roy, joined by Governor Burns,

THE FIRST DISNEYLAND AMBASSADOR, JULIE REIHM

GREAT MOMENTS WITH MR. LINCOLN ON MAIN STREET U.S.A.

THE SITE FOR WALT DISNEY WORLD

CLEARING THE LAND IN FLORIDA

WALT AND ROY JOIN THE GOVERNOR OF FLORIDA TO ANNOUNCE WALT DISNEY WORLD

(AT LEFT) HAYLEY MILLS WITH D.C. IN *THAT DARN CAT!;* (AT RIGHT) ANNETTE FUNICELLO IN *THE MONKEY'S UNCLE*

publicly announced their plans to build Walt Disney World.

During 1965, due to Walt's preoccupation with the new Florida theme park and the World's Fair, the Studio released the smallest number of features since 1957. Hayley Mills and Dean Jones starred in *That Darn Cat!*, the story of a frisky feline named D.C. (short for "Darn Cat"), who is the key to an FBI kidnapping investigation. This classic Disney comedy marked Hayley's final Disney feature film appearance. Also released by the studio was *Those Calloways*, starring

Brian Keith, and *The Monkey's Uncle*, starring Tommy Kirk and Annette Funicello, also in her final Disney theatrical role. *The Monkey's Uncle* also marked the motion picture debut of the tremendously popular band, The Beach Boys, singing the film's title song with Annette. In addition, the steady stream of profits from *Mary Poppins* enabled the company to report over $100 million in gross income for the first time.

☆1966

Walt Disney rang in New Year 1966 as the Grand Marshal of the annual Tournament of Roses parade in Pasadena, California. To the millions of people watching, Walt looked much the same as he did on his weekly television series. But Walt was facing increasing health problems and illnesses, which he managed to

WALT DISNEY SERVES AS GRAND MARSHAL FOR THE TOURNAMENT OF ROSES PARADE

keep quiet from his employees, stockholders and the world. To nearly everyone around him, it was business as usual on the Disney lot.

During the year, several additions were made at Disneyland Park, beginning with the dedication of It's a Small World in Fantasyland. The Primeval World Diorama opened as well and could be viewed while riding the Disneyland Railroad.

In July, Walt Disney dedicated Disneyland's first new themed "land," New Orleans Square. The 3-acre, $18-million expansion captured the beauty and charm of the 19th-century French Quarter.

PRIMEVAL WORLD AT DISNEYLAND

NEW ORLEANS SQUARE AT DISNEYLAND

IT'S A SMALL WORLD IN FANTASYLAND

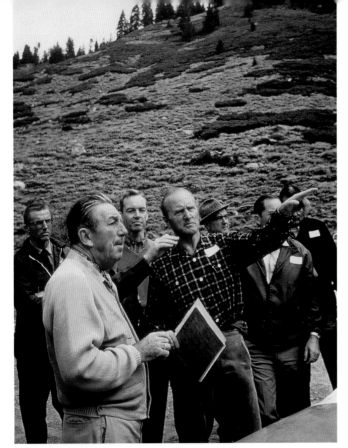

WALT DISNEY AT MINERAL KING

CONCEPT ART FOR MINERAL KING RESORT

FRED MACMURRAY IN
FOLLOW ME, BOYS!

Walt Disney entered a bid to develop a resort area at Mineral King, which the government gladly accepted. The area was located in the Sierra Nevada Mountains of California, and the U. S. Government had recently opened it to private development. However, Walt's plans were quickly put to a halt when critics and environmentalists felt that the beautiful, untouched land would be desecrated. Disney tried to convince skeptics that he would enhance the area, enabling more people to enjoy its beauty, but the critics won out. Congress eventually voted to turn Mineral King into part of Sequoia National Park, and no private development would be permitted.

Meanwhile, the Studio sent four films into the theaters in 1966: *The Ugly Dachshund, Lt. Robin Crusoe U.S.N., The Fighting Prince of Donegal* and *Follow Me, Boys!*, which marked the Disney motion picture debut of actor Kurt Russell. Disney also presented *Winnie the Pooh and the*

WINNIE THE POOH AND THE HONEY TREE

Honey Tree, its first animated featurette based on A. A. Milne's popular children's books. The film featured the loveable Pooh and all his friends from the Hundred Acre Wood, with Pooh encountering a swarm of bees and a wonderful honey tree.

The year was a busy one for Walt. Not only was he involved in the current live-action film program and in taping introductions for the TV shows, but he was holding meetings on *The Jungle Book* and deep in planning the Florida project, a pirate attraction and updates to Tomorrowland at Disneyland, as well as the plans for a ski resort at Mineral King. In October he was presented with the prestigious Showman of the Year award by the National Association of Theater Owners. But his health slowly declined, and at nine-thirty in the morning on December 15, ten days after his 65th birthday, Walt Disney died of an acute circulatory collapse at St. Joseph's Hospital across the street from the Disney Studio in Burbank.

In newspapers and on radio and television around the globe were reports of Walt Disney's death. The world was shocked and saddened by what it heard. The *Los Angeles Times* said of Walt, "No man in show business has left a richer legacy," and the *New York Times* reported, "...Walt Disney became one of Hollywood's master entrepreneurs and one of the world's greatest entertainers.... He was, in short, a legend in his own lifetime." Former President Eisenhower said, "He touched a common chord in all humanity. We shall not soon see his

like again." From kings, queens and presidents to children everywhere, the world mourned the loss of Walt Disney. It had truly lost a great pioneer, artist, storyteller, father, innovator and creative mind.

As Walt had requested, the day after his death his body was cremated and his immediate family gathered for a simple funeral service at Forest Lawn Memorial Park in Glendale. The news was a tremendous blow to the four thousand men and women who worked at the Studio, Disneyland and Disney offices around the world, but Roy O. Disney stepped up, taking the helm at Walt Disney Productions. In a statement regarding the death of Walt, Roy assured employees, stockholders and the public that he and the creative team assembled by his brother would continue to build upon the fantastic legacy that was started nearly forty years earlier.

THE WORLD MOURNED THE DEATH OF WALT DISNEY

Even with the loss of its founder, Walt Disney Productions continued to grow, opening new attractions at Disneyland, releasing new slates of motion pictures into the theaters and moving forward on the Walt Disney World project in Florida. A new era had begun in the history of Disney—an era without Walt.

1967 was filled with grand openings at Disneyland. New Orleans Square's premiere attraction, Pirates of the Caribbean, debuted with great

PIRATES OF THE CARIBBEAN

NEWLY
RENOVATED
TOMORROWLAND
AT DISNEYLAND

fanfare, introducing guests to an amazing voyage with the saltiest band of buccaneers ever to sail the Spanish Main. Resting along the waters of Pirates of the Caribbean, the Blue Bayou Restaurant opened, offering fine dining in a moonlit Louisiana bayou setting.

After a $23-million renovation, an all-new Tomorrowland opened in July. The Carousel of Progress opened after its run at the New York World's Fair. Taking guests on a leisurely ride through Tomorrowland was the new PeopleMover. The attraction's electric motors embedded in the track propelled the vehicles, and, for 1967, the technology was considered to be quite innovative. Also opening in Tomorrowland were Flight to the Moon and Adventure Thru Inner Space, in which guests boarded "Atomobiles" and were transported through a gigantic microscope to see what the inside of an atom might be like. In addition, the popular Circle-Vision film, *America*

AMERICA THE BEAUTIFUL IN CIRCLE-VISION 360

(ABOVE) KING LOUIE AND BALOO IN *THE JUNGLE BOOK;* (AT RIGHT) KING LOUIE AND THE APES; (BELOW) MOWGLI AND BALOO

the Beautiful, was reshot for the land's reopening.

On May 30, site preparation began on the Walt Disney World project, requiring swamp drainage, clearing of land, removal of tree stumps and much more. The Florida legislature created the Reedy Creek Improvement District, a quasi-governmental entity, to regulate the Walt Disney World property. The new district had its own building codes, supervised construction projects, managed wildlife preservation and even ran the fire department.

The *Jungle Book*, one of Walt Disney's crowning achievements and the last animated feature produced under his guidance, was received with open arms by theater audiences. The film became one of Disney's all-time box

(AT LEFT) *SCROOGE McDUCK AND MONEY;* (AT RIGHT) *MONKEYS, GO HOME!*

E. CARDON "CARD" WALKER

office winners. The *Jungle Book* followed the adventures of Mowgli, a man cub who is raised in the jungle and becomes friends with Baloo the bear and Bagheera the panther. Mowgli crosses paths with a host of unsavory characters including Kaa, King Louie, and Shere Khan, who has vowed to kill the man cub. Also in animation, the special cartoon featurette, *Scrooge McDuck and Money*, was released, marking the character's theatrical debut.

In the live-action arena, the Studio released *Monkeys, Go Home!*, *The Adventures of Bullwhip Griffin*, *The Happiest Millionaire*, *The Gnome-Mobile* and *Charlie, the Lonesome Cougar*. Starring Fred MacMurray, Tommy Steele, Lesley Ann Warren in her feature film debut and Greer Garson in her final motion picture appearance, *The Happiest Millionaire* was the Disney Studio's most lavish musical production since *Mary Poppins*, and the last live-action film touched by Walt.

Without Walt, the company turned to E. Cardon "Card" Walker, executive vice president of operations, to supervise film production, along with a staff of seven key producers—Bill Anderson, Bill Walsh, Winston Hibler, James Algar, Ron Miller, Harry Tytle and Roy E. Disney. These eight men would be primarily responsible for handling the Studio's film production efforts over the next decade.

In 1968, Mickey Mouse celebrated his 40th birthday with a television special on *The Wonderful World of Disney* and in a major *Life* magazine article. The interest in Mickey Mouse spawned by the anniversary celebrations led to the reintroduction of a wristwatch with Mickey on the face—a product that had been on hiatus for almost a decade. This time, however, adults were wearing Mickey Mouse watches along with their kids. Rising interest in nostalgia soon had collectors beginning to search out old Mickey memorabilia, starting a Disneyana craze that would continue to the present day.

Four feature films were distributed by the Studio in 1968. Peter Ustinov and Dean Jones teamed up in the hit comedy *Blackbeard's Ghost*, with Ustinov lending his irreverent flamboyance to the role of the bloodthirsty Blackbeard. *The One and Only, Genuine, Original Family Band*, which told the story of the 11-member Bower family band as they prepared to perform at the Democratic Presidential Convention for Grover Cleveland, was based on the autobiographical novel by Laura Bower Van Nuys. Also released were *Never a Dull Moment* and *The Horse in the Gray Flannel Suit*.

Winnie the Pooh and the Blustery Day, the second animated featurette to star the world-famous teddy bear, was released. During the course of the film, in which a blustery day turns into a storm, Pooh and Piglet get washed away by a flood, and Owl loses his home. In one particularly imaginative sequence, Pooh's nightmares are overrun by a frighteningly fantastic band of creatures known as Heffalumps and Woozles. The featurette would win the Academy Award for Best Cartoon Short Subject.

THE ONE AND ONLY, GENUINE, ORIGINAL FAMILY BAND

PETER USTINOV AND DEAN JONES IN *BLACKBEARD'S GHOST*

DEAN JONES IN *THE HORSE IN THE GRAY FLANNEL SUIT*

WINNIE THE POOH AND THE BLUSTERY DAY

DONN TATUM

Meanwhile, the U.S. Postal Service introduced a new postage stamp honoring Walt Disney. This was the first-ever Disney-themed postage stamp. In later years, Disney characters would appear on numerous stamps internationally.

Elsewhere at Disney, Roy O. Disney retired as president of Walt Disney Productions in favor of Donn B. Tatum, but did remain chairman of the board. Roy's intention was to devote more time to the Florida project, especially with respect to financial planning.

In Florida, the company laid the foundation for the massive Walt Disney World project. More than 1.5 million cubic yards of earth were moved, broad lagoons were created, 38 miles of water control channels were built and the elevation had to be raised in some areas of the property such as the Magic Kingdom site. A total of 2,500 acres of land was made ready for development while master planning proceeded at WED Enterprises in California.

☆1969

For years, a Haunted Mansion sat empty along the Rivers of America at Disneyland. Disney designers could not decide what to put inside. Some Imagineers lobbied for an ominous and scary attraction with an exterior in drastic disrepair, while others insisted on a stately manor that would offer a light-hearted look at the immortal. Walt Disney, of course, had made the final decision, opting for an elegant exterior, and saying he would let the ghosts take care of the inside.

The result was a beautiful southern mansion, in which guests would

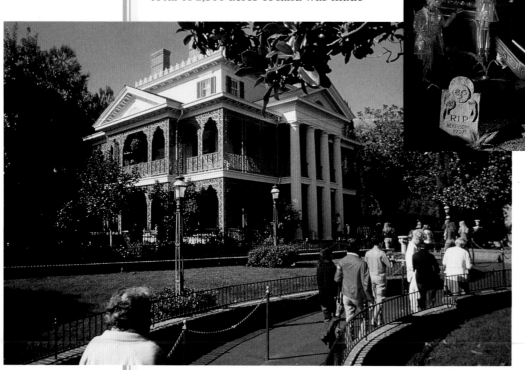

THE HAUNTED MANSION IN NEW ORLEANS SQUARE

(AT LEFT) THE APOLLO 11 MOON LANDING IS VIEWED BY DISNEYLAND GUESTS; (AT RIGHT) PRESIDENT NIXON PRESENTS LILLY DISNEY WITH A MEDAL HONORING HER HUSBAND

board "doom buggies" and encounter a band of frighteningly funny ghosts, ghouls and goblins. In August, the Haunted Mansion finally opened to eager crowds in New Orleans Square with its assemblage of 999 happy haunts beginning their eternal graveyard revelry.

On August 12, 1966, Disneyland televised the historic Apollo 11 moon landing on the Tomorrowland Stage. Also at Disneyland, Love Bug Day was held to help promote the newly released Disney film, *The Love Bug*.

Also on the theme park front, progress was being made in Florida on the Walt Disney World project, with April marking the beginning of actual construction on the Magic Kingdom and the resort hotels. Also in April, Disney held a major press conference, detailing the plans for the project.

The Studio's first film of the year was *The Love Bug*, which ended up being the highest-grossing movie in the United States for 1969. Featuring Herbie, the spunky little Volkswagen, and a cast including Dean Jones, Michele Lee, David Tomlinson, Buddy Hackett and Andy Granatelli, the

DEAN JONES IN
THE LOVE BUG

LOVE BUG DAY AT DISNEYLAND

BILLY MUMY IN
RASCAL

KURT RUSSELL IN
*THE COMPUTER
WORE TENNIS
SHOES*

IT'S TOUGH TO BE A BIRD

film's success eventually led to three theatrical sequels. Other films released this year were *Smith!*, *Rascal* and the Kurt Russell comedy, *The Computer Wore Tennis Shoes*.

The special live-action and cartoon featurette *It's Tough to Be a Bird* was also released and would win the Academy Award for Best Short Subject of 1969.

1970

During 1970 the Disney organization was primarily focusing its energies and resources on the Walt Disney World Resort, which was now only a year away from its opening.

WALT DISNEY WORLD PREVIEW CENTER

MAGIC KINGDOM CONSTRUCTION
AT WALT DISNEY WORLD

THE ARISTOCATS

For this reason, the Studio's film and television output remained minimal. In June, the Walt Disney World Preview Center opened in nearby Lake Buena Vista, showcasing large models, paintings and drawings of the new vacation destination. Hundreds of thousands of people visited the center to catch a glimpse of what was in store for them in 1971.

Meanwhile, the original Disney park celebrated its 15th anniversary with a spectacular summer celebration that was attended by more than 5 million guests. After steady yearly increases, Disneyland hit an annual attendance record, with more than 10 million guests visiting the Park for the first year ever. The company was also able to take over as general contractor for the Walt Disney World project, largely due to its greatly expanded engineering and construction organization, WED Enterprises.

In 1970 Disney released *The Aristocats*, its first animated feature com-

pleted without Walt's guiding hand. Live-action offerings for the year were *King of the Grizzlies* and *The Boatniks*. The special cartoon featurette *Dad, Can I Borrow the Car?* was also released.

EDGAR THE BUTLER IN *THE ARISTOCATS*

THE WALT DISNEY ARCHIVES

On June 22, the Walt Disney Archives was established and charged with recording and preserving the history of Disney, including historical documents, memorabilia, selected film and theme park props and other items pertaining to Walt Disney, his family and the Disney company as a whole.

☆1971

Six years had passed since Walt and Roy joined Florida governor Haydon Burns at the press conference to officially announce their Walt Disney World project. Since that time, thousands of people dedicated hundreds of thousands of hours moving tons of earth, pumping millions of gallons of water, passing three pieces of legislation, cutting miles of red tape, interviewing the 6,200 opening crew cast members and building an entire kingdom out of Florida swampland. $400 million later, the result was the opening of Walt Disney World on October 1, 1971. The new resort was Disney's second and largest theme park, and would soon become the world's most popular vacation destination.

Since Walt's death, Roy O. Disney spearheaded every aspect of the Walt Disney World project from development and engineering to construction and opening. He closely guided the new park's evolution, making certain that his brother's vision was carried out. On October 25, the day of the park's official dedication ceremony, Roy stood in Town Square at the Magic Kingdom with Mickey Mouse, surrounded by celebrities, special

ROY O. DISNEY AND MICKEY MOUSE DEDICATE WALT DISNEY WORLD

THANKSGIVING TRAFFIC JAM LEADING TO WALT DISNEY WORLD

CINDERELLA CASTLE UNDER CONSTRUCTION

MAIN STREET CONSTRUCTION

CONTEMPORARY RESORT UNDER CONSTRUCTION

guests, family and employees to pay one final tribute to his partner and brother, Walt. Roy said, "Walt Disney World is a tribute to the philosophy and life of Walter Elias Disney... and to the talents, the dedication and the loyalty of the entire Disney organization that made Walt Disney's dream come true."

The main attraction of the Walt Disney World Resort was the Magic Kingdom, which was quite similar to Disney's flagship park in California. Its six themed "lands," Main Street, U.S.A., Adventureland, Frontierland Liberty Square, Fantasyland and Tomorrowland, included several attractions that were unique to the Magic Kingdom. In Frontierland was the Country Bear Jamboree with its lively musical cast of *Audio-Animatronics* bears. Liberty Square was

WALT DISNEY WORLD GRAND OPENING

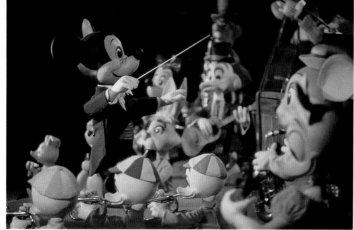

MICKEY MOUSE REVUE

COUNTRY BEAR
JAMBOREE

20,000 LEAGUES UNDER THE SEA ATTRACTION IN FANTASYLAND

CINDERELLA CASTLE MOSAICS

home to The Hall of Presidents, an *Audio-Animatronics* presentation saluting all the presidents of the United States.

Two Fantasyland attractions, Mickey Mouse Revue and 20,000 Leagues Under the Sea, could also be found only in the Magic Kingdom. The former was another *Audio-Animatronics* musical attraction with a large cast of Disney characters performing a selection of popular Disney songs. 20,000 Leagues Under the Sea quickly became one of the park's most popular attractions. Differing from the Disneyland submarines which were inspired by the United States' nuclear fleet of the 1950s, those at Walt Disney World were replicas of Captain Nemo's *Nautilus,* the fanciful vessel depicted in the classic 1954 Disney film.

Soaring high above the Magic Kingdom was the majestic Cinderella Castle, the spires of which reached 189 feet into the sky. It was distinctively larger and more ornate than Sleeping Beauty Castle at Disneyland. In fact, a large restaurant, King Stefan's Banquet Hall, occupied the second story of the castle. Of course, no one could explain why King Stefan from *Sleeping Beauty* had a banquet hall in Cinderella's castle—the problem would not be rectified until 1997 when the restaurant was renamed Cinderella's Royal Table.

In addition to the Magic Kingdom, Walt Disney World included golf courses, lakes and lagoons for fishing and watersports and two resort

hotels—the Contemporary Hotel and the Polynesian Hotel.

For good reason, the year was slow at Disneyland, with most Disney efforts focusing on Florida. One new attraction, however, the Davy Crockett Explorer Canoes, was added. On June 17, Valerie Suldo became the Park's 100-millionth guest.

Five new films were released. The most elaborate, *Bedknobs and Broomsticks*, was the classic story of eccentric spinster Eglantine Price, whose study of witchcraft enabled her to find a magic formula that would defeat the Nazis and help England win World War II. The film had an outlandish budget and fantastic special effects, but did not make a big splash at the box office. It won the Oscar for Best Visual Effects and was nominated for Best Art Direction/Set Direction, Best

Song ("The Age of Not Believing"), Best Scoring and Best Costume Design.

The $1,000,000 Duck, about a white duck that lays golden eggs, starring veteran Disney actor Dean Jones and actress Sandy Duncan in her feature

DAVID TOMLINSON IN *BEDKNOBS AND BROOMSTICKS*

113

DEAN JONES IN *THE $1,000,000 DUCK*

KURT RUSSELL IN *THE BAREFOOT EXECUTIVE*

THE WILD COUNTRY

BRIAN KEITH IN *SCANDALOUS JOHN*

film debut, was also released. Kurt Russell starred in *The Barefoot Executive*, in which his character, who works at a failing television network, discovers a chimpanzee who has an uncanny knack for choosing hit programs. *Scandalous John* was the rip-snorting tale of an old rancher who takes off on a cattle drive and does battle with a wealthy, land-grabbing industrialist. *The Wild Country* chronicled the hardships faced by an eastern family that moves to a broken-down Wyoming homestead.

On December 20, Roy O. Disney died at the age of 78. After Walt's death, Roy had dedicated the rest of his life to seeing his brother's final dream, Walt Disney World, become a reality. With the loss of Walt and Roy Disney,

the board of directors, for the first time, had to turn outside the Disney family for leadership of the company. Donn Tatum, who was previously the company's president, was selected as chairman, and executive vice president and chief operating officer Card Walker became president.

1972

Disneyland Park began one of the most cherished traditions in its history as the Main Street Electrical Parade illuminated the Park's parade route for the first time in 1972. The immensely popular entertainment extravaganza would attract record crowds during summer evenings for a quarter of a century.

Disneyland opened its seventh themed "land," Bear Country. Themed to a rustic forest in America's Pacific Northwest, the area was home to the Country Bear Jamboree, which was the first Disneyland attraction to have originated at Walt Disney World.

Actress Jodie Foster made her motion picture debut in *Napoleon and Samantha*, the story of two children who journey into the mountains to find a safe home for their gentle pet lion. Other films released into theaters were *The Biscuit Eater; Now You See Him, Now You Don't,* starring Kurt Russell as Medfield College student Dexter Reilly; *Run, Cougar, Run;* and *Snowball Express,* featuring Dean Jones. For the first time in 16 years, *Song of the South* was re-released into theaters, becoming the highest-grossing reissue in Disney history.

In 1972, *The Mouse Factory* syndicated television series made its debut. The program combined classic Disney cartoons with special live-action guest appearances by celebrities like Dom De Luise, Don Knotts, Phyllis Diller, Jim Backus, Kurt Russell, Ken Berry and Annette Funicello.

The world-famous Sothebys™ auction house held the first ever "Disneyana" auction, and Disney Consumer Products introduced the backwards Goofy watch, with the numbers backward on the face and the hands running counterclockwise. It was an instant hit in stores.

MAIN STREET ELECTRICAL PARADE AT DISNEYLAND

COUNTRY BEAR JAMBOREE ENTRANCE IN BEAR COUNTRY

THE MOUSE FACTORY

IN THIS PRESIDENTIAL ELECTION YEAR, A POOH FOR PRESIDENT EVENT WAS HELD AT DISNEYLAND

ROBIN HOOD AND LITTLE JOHN

MAID MARIAN IN *ROBIN HOOD*

ROBIN HOOD AND PRINCE JOHN

☆1973

On October 16, 1973, Walt Disney Productions celebrated its 50th anniversary. As it reached its half-century mark, the Studio released five new features. First Disney retold the classic tale of one of England's legendary rogues in its latest animated feature, *Robin Hood*. In this version, however, Robin and Maid Marian were foxes, Little John a bear, Friar Tuck a badger and Prince John an arrogant yet sniveling lion. In *The World's Greatest Athlete*, Nanu, a boy raised by a tribe in Africa, is brought to America so that he can use his extraordinary athletic abilities to help a college win an NCAA track and field event. Veteran Disney actor Fred Mac-Murray played his final role at Disney in *Charley and the Angel*, and James

Garner played his first as an army deserter who befriends a 10-year-old Indian boy in *One Little Indian*. *Superdad*, starring Bob Crane, Kurt Russell and Barbara Rush, was also released.

The Walt Disney Story opened on Main Street at both Disneyland and the Walt Disney World Magic Kingdom. The attraction featured a film narrated by Walt himself that told his life story. In Anaheim, included was an exact reproduction of Walt Disney's offices from the Disney Studios in Burbank, along with the other historical memorabilia and awards.

JAN-MICHAEL VINCENT AND FRIEND IN *THE WORLD'S GREATEST ATHLETE*

FRED MACMURRAY AND HARRY MORGAN IN *CHARLEY AND THE ANGEL*

JAMES GARNER IN *ONE LITTLE INDIAN*

KURT RUSSELL, BOB CRANE AND KATHLEEN CODY IN *SUPERDAD*

(ABOVE LEFT) MICKEY MOUSE AND LILLIAN DISNEY DEDICATE THE WALT DISNEY STORY AT DISNEYLAND; (AT LEFT) THE WALT DISNEY STORY

PIRATES OF THE
CARIBBEAN AT WALT
DISNEY WORLD

PATRICK WAYNE IN *THE BEARS AND I*

The Richard F. Irvine Riverboat made its inaugural voyage down the Rivers of America in the Magic Kingdom at Walt Disney World. The authentic steamboat was named for Dick Irvine, one of the early Disney designers and one of the first executives at WED Enterprises. Also opening was the Pirates of the Caribbean attraction in Adventureland at Walt Disney World.

The original version of the attraction had opened six years earlier at Disneyland Park, and its popularity there had created a demand for a similar attraction in Florida. The Golf Resort hotel was opened at Walt Disney World, catering to those who enjoyed its secluded location and close proximity to the resort's golf courses.

1974

Herbie Rides Again, the first of three sequels to the hit 1969 comedy *The Love Bug,* raced into theaters in 1974 as did *The Bears and I* and *The Castaway Cowboy. The Island at the Top of the World,* a film partially shot in Arctic Circle regions of Alaska,

HERBIE RIDES
AGAIN

THE HYPERION AIRSHIP FROM *THE ISLAND AT THE TOP OF THE WORLD*

Greenland and Norway, chronicles the adventures of a wealthy Englishman who commissions an expedition to search the Arctic for his missing son.

In animation, a special featurette, *Winnie the Pooh and Tigger Too*, was released. In this installment of the stories based on A.A. Milne's writings, there is a problem in the Hundred Acre Wood—Tigger's bouncing has been getting on everyone's nerves. Eventually Tigger bounces into a very tall tree and needs to be rescued, but must first agree never to bounce again. The film was nominated as Best Animated Short Film by the Academy.

America Sings opened in Tomorrowland at Disneyland Park, using the carousel theater that originally housed the Carousel of Progress. Sam the Eagle was the host of this toe-tapping journey through the history of American popular music. The attraction featured four eras of music and utilized over 100 *Audio-Animatronics* characters. In Tomorrowland at Walt Disney World, the *Magic Carpet 'Round the World* Circle-Vision film premiered.

In the meantime, on the international scene, Disney executives held their first talks regarding the possible construction of a Disneyland-like theme park in Japan. Executives also realized the growing interest in the collecting of Disney memorabilia, so the Company agreed to assist in the publication of Cecil Munsey's book *Disneyana: Walt Disney Collectibles*, which detailed the history of Disney merchandising.

(CLOCKWISE FROM LEFT) *WINNIE THE POOH AND TIGGER TOO;* TREASURE ISLAND, A WILDLIFE SANCTUARY, OPENED AT WALT DISNEY WORLD; AMERICA SINGS AT DISNEYLAND

"There's really no secret about our approach. We keep moving forward— opening up new doors and doing new things— because we're curious."

WALT DISNEY

Disney was clearly on its way to regaining its status as a major force in the entertainment industry.

AMERICA ON PARADE

1975

In celebration of the Bicentennial of the United States, both Disneyland and Walt Disney World presented America on Parade. The patriotic tribute told the story of America's history, culture and achievements from the days of its forefathers to the present. The parade featured a special medley of popular American songs played on a historic band organ and was led by Mickey, Donald and Goofy dressed as the "Spirit of '76."

CARD WALKER WITH EPCOT MODEL

In 1975, Disney President Card Walker announced the Company's plans to build EPCOT Center. The WEDway PeopleMover attraction and Space Mountain opened in Tomorrowland in the Magic Kingdom at Walt Disney World. Adding to the Park's appeal, especially for younger guests, the high-speed Space Mountain attraction was the first thrill ride

SPACE MOUNTAIN

constructed at the Magic Kingdom. Since it was totally in the dark, the ride was unique in that passengers were unable to anticipate its twists and turns.

Since man had landed on the moon, the Flight to the Moon attraction had become outdated and had to be replaced. Mission to Mars therefore opened in Tomorrowland at both Disneyland and Walt Disney World.

Great Moments with Mr. Lincoln, which had been missing from Disneyland Park since the *Walt Disney Story* film took its place, returned due to popular demand, and the Carousel of Progress opened at Walt Disney World, featuring a new theme song, "The Best Time of Your Life." Also opening was Lake Buena Vista Village, a cluster of shops along a lagoon at Walt Disney World.

MISSION TO MARS AT DISNEYLAND

LAKE BUENA VISTA VILLAGE

In the movies, actor Kurt Russell played the role of college student Dexter Reilly for the third time in *The Strongest Man in the World*. In *Escape to Witch Mountain*, orphans Tony and Tia Malone, who are actually castaways from a distant universe, use their psychic powers to find their uncle and go home. The mining town of Quake City, California, is shaken up as never before when three mischievous orphans and two inept outlaws, played by Don Knotts and Tim Conway, cause all sorts of trouble in *The Apple Dumpling Gang*. Also

FLOYD GOTTFREDSON

released was *One of Our Dinosaurs Is Missing,* the story of a British intelligence agent who hides top-secret microfilm in a dinosaur skeleton.

Artist Floyd Gottfredson retired in 1975 after drawing the Mickey Mouse comic strip for 45 years. In addition to drawing the daily Mickey Mouse strip, he wrote it from 1930 to 1932 and served as the head of the Comic Strip Department from 1930 to 1946. The retirement of Gottfredson and many other key artists would soon create a problem for the Studio, as there was no ongoing training program in place to prepare their successors. It would take nearly a decade for the Animation Department to completely recover from the retirees' departure.

Walt Disney Productions released five films in 1976. *Ride a Wild Pony* was the first Disney feature filmed in Australia, *Treasure of Matecumbe,* a post-Civil-War-era treasure hunt adventure, was the first produc-

KURT RUSSELL IN *THE STRONGEST MAN IN THE WORLD*

IKE EISENMANN AND KIM RICHARDS IN *ESCAPE TO WITCH MOUNTAIN*

tion to have scenes filmed on the Walt Disney World property and *The Shaggy D.A.* was the first and only theatrical sequel to the classic 1959 Disney comedy, *The Shaggy Dog.*

The 50-millionth guest, Susan Brummer, passed through the turnstiles of the Magic Kingdom at Walt Disney World, while River Country, an old-fashioned swimming-hole-style water park, opened adjacent to the Fort Wilderness campground. At Disneyland Park, the Disneyana Shop opened on Main Street, offering a special selection of rare Disney merchandise and collectibles.

Disney aired a Bicentennial television special entitled *America on Parade,* which was hosted by the legendary comedian Red Skelton, and Bob Thomas's popular biography, *Walt Disney: An American Original,* was published.

DISNEYANA SHOP MERCHANDISE

(CLOCKWISE) ROBERT BETTLES IN *RIDE A WILD PONY;* TIM CONWAY IN *THE SHAGGY D.A;* BOB THOMAS'S *WALT DISNEY: AN AMERICAN ORIGINAL;* RIVER COUNTRY AT WALT DISNEY WORLD

BERNARD, BIANCA AND EVINRUDE IN *THE RESCUERS*

☆1977☁

For the first time since the 1940 release of both *Pinocchio* and *Fantasia,* Disney presented two animated features in a single year, when *The Rescuers* and *The Many Adventures of Winnie the Pooh* premiered in 1977. Bernard and Bianca, two mice representing the Rescue Aid Society, rush to save a little orphan girl named Penny from evil kidnappers in *The Rescuers. The Many Adventures of Winnie the Pooh* was actually a compilation of three previously released Winnie the Pooh featurettes.

Disney also produced four live-action films in 1977, starting with Jodie Foster as Annabel Andrews, a 13-year-old who wishes she could trade places with her mother and finds that wish come true on a *Freaky Friday.* The film was based on the popular book by Mary Rodgers. *The Littlest Horse Thieves,* in which three kids try to save the lives of a

Yorkshire coal mine's pit ponies that are being replaced by more efficient machinery, and the second sequel to *The Love Bug, Herbie Goes to Monte Carlo,* were released. The popular musical comedy *Pete's Dragon* also premiered, combining live-action with the animated dragon Elliott, whose mischievous nature causes all sorts of chaos in the small Maine fishing town of Passamaquoddy.

Meanwhile, over at the theme parks, two years after the opening of the original Space Mountain roller coaster attraction at Walt Disney World, a second one

ELLIOTT FROM *PETE'S DRAGON*

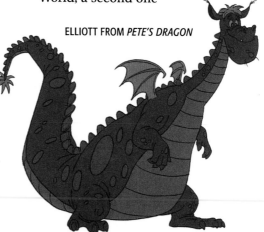

126

THE *EMPRESS LILLY* AT LAKE BUENA VISTA VILLAGE

opened in Tomorrowland at Disneyland. Disneyland also debuted the new Very Merry Christmas Parade, with dancing Christmas trees and snowmen, marching toy soldiers, skating snowflakes and of course a special appearance by Santa Claus.

At Walt Disney World, the *Empress Lilly*, a riverboat docked alongside Lake Buena Vista Village, opened. Named after Walt Disney's wife, Lillian, the *Empress Lilly* housed three restaurants: the Fisherman's Deck, the Steerman's Quarters and the elegant Empress Room, which became the most exclusive restaurant on the Walt Disney World property.

On the television front, in an effort to appeal to contemporary kids, a new Mickey Mouse Club series was released in television syndication with twelve new Mouseketeers. Besides being produced in color, a major change in the program was that the daily themes were changed—Monday was Who, What, Why, Where, When and How Day; Tuesday was Let's Go Day; Wednesday was Surprise Day; Thursday was Discovery Day; and Friday was Showtime Day.

VERY MERRY CHRISTMAS PARADE AT DISNEYLAND

MICKEY MOUSE CLUB

JODIE FOSTER AND HELEN HAYES IN *CANDLESHOE*

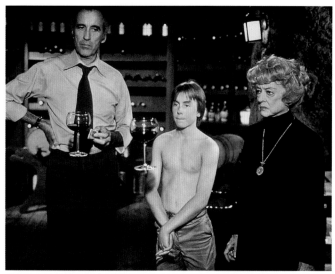

CHRISTOPHER LEE, IKE EISENMANN AND BETTE DAVIS IN *RETURN FROM WITCH MOUNTAIN*

1978

Candleshoe, starring Jodie Foster as a street-smart tomboy from Los Angeles who poses as the long-lost heiress to a stately English manor, was Disney's first film release in 1978. *Return from Witch Mountain* brought Tony and Tia back to Earth for a vacation, but Tony is kidnapped by a sinister scientist and Tia must save the day. In *The Cat from Outer Space*, Ken Berry starred as a quirky physicist who helps an extraterrestrial cat named Jake fix his spaceship. In *Hot Lead and Cold Feet*, twin brothers Eli and Wild Billy compete against each other in a fast-paced race to win possession of the rickety Old West town their father founded. Disney also released a special Christmas animated featurette *The Small One*, the heartwarming story of a boy who sells his beloved donkey to a kind couple, Mary and Joseph, who are on their way to Bethlehem.

JAKE IN *THE CAT FROM OUTER SPACE*

THE SMALL ONE

THE SMALL ONE

Mickey Mouse celebrated his 50th birthday in 1978 with the television special *Mickey's 50*, during which dozens of celebrities offer the world-famous superstar their best birthday wishes. Mickey was also given his own star on the Hollywood Walk of Fame and was recognized on a special cover of *Life* magazine.

At Disneyland after a brief renovation, the Matterhorn Bobsleds attraction reopened. It now utilized a new ride system with tandem bobsleds, as well as a newly added ice cavern, glowing ice crystals and a fierce Abominable Snowman.

Walt Disney's legendary Nine Old Men (Walt's nine top animators in the 1940s, whom he had likened to the "Nine Old Men" on President Franklin D. Roosevelt's Supreme Court) were honored with a Pioneers in Film award at the University of Southern California, presented by Delta Kappa Alpha, the national honorary cinema fraternity.

THE ABOMINABLE SNOWMAN IN THE MATTERHORN

BIG THUNDER MOUNTAIN RAILROAD AT DISNEYLAND

GROUNDBREAKING FOR EPCOT CENTER

EPCOT CENTER RENDERING

1979

In 1979, Disneyland Park opened its newest E ticket attraction, Big Thunder Mountain Railroad in Frontierland. Billed as "the wildest ride in the wilderness," this rickety mine train loses control, taking guests careening through dark caverns swarming with bats, into deep sandstone gorges and through abandoned mines.

Groundbreaking ceremonies were held for EPCOT Center, the second theme park at Walt Disney World. It would have its grand opening in the fall of 1982. At the Magic Kingdom, Kurt Miller, Walt Disney World's 100-millionth guest, passed through the turnstiles on October 22.

In theaters a total of four films were released by the Studio during the year. The first was *The North Avenue Irregulars*, the story of a minister and his group of devoted church ladies who go undercover to expose organized crime in their hometown. Tim Conway and Don Knotts gave an encore performance as the bumbling Theodore and Amos in *The Apple Dumpling Gang Rides Again*. In *Unidentified Flying Oddball*, an astronaut accidentally flies back in time to the age of King Arthur in this modernization of the Mark Twain classic *A Connecticut Yankee in King Arthur's Court*. Finally, after five years in development, 14 months in production and a cost of

$20 million, *The Black Hole* was released, amazing audiences with its dazzling special effects.

Of the seven major studios in Hollywood, Disney's box office share was the lowest at 4 percent, and Disney saw its lowest film profits in a decade. Even reissues of *The Love Bug, Bedknobs and Broomsticks, 101 Dalmatians* and *Sleeping Beauty* could not bolster film revenue.

While few new television programs were created, *Disney's Wonderful World,* the newest title given to the Disney television anthology series, began its run in September on NBC. The program primarily aired theatrical movies in two parts and reruns.

⭐1980

Card Walker was elevated from president to chairman of the board of Walt Disney Productions, and Ron Miller was elected president in 1980.

The Studio released a total of three films this year: *Midnight Madness, The Last Flight of Noah's Ark* and *Herbie Goes Bananas. Midnight Madness,* the story about a college student who organizes an all-night treasure hunt, was the first film produced and released by Disney without the Disney name. By removing the Disney label, the Studio hoped that the film would

HERBIE GOES BANANAS

RON MILLER AND CARD WALKER

BUENA VISTA HOME VIDEO RELEASES ITS FIRST CASSETTES

TOD AND COPPER IN
*THE FOX AND THE
HOUND*

reach teens and young adults, who tended to stay away from the family-oriented "Disney" films.

Disney also released its first videos through its newly established Buena Vista Home Video unit. The first releases were compilations of popular Disney cartoons and a selection of live-action films.

Elsewhere, groundbreaking took place at Tokyo Disneyland, and Goofy became the mascot of the French Olympic team. Walt Disney World opened its Big Thunder Mountain Railroad attraction in Frontierland—Big Thunder was the first major attraction to debut at the Magic Kingdom since Space Mountain in 1974, because most of the construction effort at Walt Disney World was being expended on building EPCOT Center.

1981

Four years after its previous animated feature, Disney released its latest, *The Fox and the Hound*, the story of two childhood friends who had no idea that they were supposed to be bitter enemies. Since most of Walt Disney's original animators had retired, this film marked the first effort by the next generation of Disney artists who would later create animated blockbusters such as *The Little Mermaid* and *Beauty and the Beast*.

The Studio's four live-action releases for 1981 were *The Devil and Max Devlin, Amy, The Watcher in the Woods* with Bette Davis and *Condorman*, which starred Michael Crawford, the man who would later become famous for playing the title role in Andrew Lloyd Webber's hit Broadway musical *The Phantom of the Opera*.

CONDORMAN

With much of the company's efforts taken up with major construction projects in Florida and Japan, there was little change at Disneyland or Walt Disney World, but Walt Disney World did celebrate its tenth anniversary with a special Tencennial Parade at the Magic Kingdom. And on January 8, Disneyland Park welcomed Gert Schelvis, its 200-millionth guest.

After negotiating with Retlaw Enterprises, the Disney family's company, Walt Disney Productions successfully purchased the rights to the Disney name. Under the terms of the agreement, the company also acquired the Disneyland Monorail and the Disneyland Railroad, both of which were previously owned and operated by Retlaw.

1982

Shortly before his death, Walt Disney had announced his plans for a utopian community to be called EPCOT (Experimental Prototype Community of Tomorrow). On October 1, 1982, that dream was realized with the opening of EPCOT Center at the Walt Disney World Resort. While Walt had originally envisioned EPCOT as a thriving metropolis with a commercial center and residential areas, the plans were redefined and it opened, at a cost of a billion dollars, as Disney's second major theme park in Florida. EPCOT Center consisted of two major sections—Future World and World Showcase.

Future World featured pavilions celebrating humankind's past achievements and explorations into the not-so-distant future. The centerpiece of Future World (and of EPCOT Center as a whole) was Spaceship Earth, an enormous, shimmering geodesic dome with 2 million feet of interior space and a diameter of 164 feet.

EPCOT CENTER GRAND OPENING

GERMANY

CANADA

THE AMERICAN ADVENTURE

THE LAND

UNIVERSE OF
ENERGY

JOURNEY INTO
IMAGINATION

Other attractions in Future World included The Land, the largest Future World pavilion, which featured agricultural, ecological and nutritional exhibits and shows; Journey Into Imagination, including the hands-on creative environment of Image Works and the 3-D film *Magic Journeys;* World of Motion, a journey through the history of transportation; Universe of Energy, utilizing two acres of solar panels that generated almost enough electricity to operate the attraction; and Communicore, featuring various exhibits, displays, restaurants and shops.

World Showcase highlighted the culture, cuisine and history of countries from around the world with elaborately detailed facades, special films, exhibits, authentic restaurants and shops with merchandise shipped to EPCOT Center from the far reaches of the globe. American Adventure, hosted by amazingly lifelike *Audio-Animatronics* figures of Benjamin Franklin and Mark Twain, served as the area's focal point, celebrating the American spirit of patriotism. Also surrounding World Showcase Lagoon were Canada, the United Kingdom, France, Italy, Japan, Germany, China and Mexico.

JAPAN   MEXICO   CHINA   ITALY

Disneyland Park rang in a new era when it replaced ticket books with its new passports, which were good for admission and unlimited use of the Park's attractions. Since the Park's first year in 1955, ticket books had always been used as admission to the theme park's attractions.

Tron, which was released this year, was the first film in motion picture history to make extensive use of computer imagery. In *Tron*, Flynn, a computer genius played by Jeff Bridges, is transported to a world where computer programs are the alter egos of the programmers who created them, only to find that he is sentenced to die on the video game grid. While

WORLD OF MOTION

BENJAMIN FRANKLIN AND MARK TWAIN IN THE AMERICAN ADVENTURE

MATT DILLON IN *TEX*

With the overwhelming success of Disneyland and Walt Disney World, executives at Disney had decided in 1980 to construct a theme park outside of the United States. Countries from around the world had approached Disney for years, encouraging them to open a park in their homelands. At the time, the most feasible option had seemed to be Japan, where the Oriental Land Company proposed the construction of a park just outside of Tokyo. Disney officials had agreed to the proposal, and work had been progressing for several years, resulting in the opening of Tokyo Disneyland on April 15, 1983.

the film was not as successful as the Studio had hoped, it did inspire a number of popular video games.

Matt Dillon starred in *Tex*, a film based on a book by best-selling teen-fiction author S. E. Hinton. Only one other feature was released during the year, *Night Crossing*, the true story of two families who risked everything, using a hot air balloon to escape from East Germany to freedom in the West.

Tokyo Disneyland was not to be an Asian version of Disneyland. The Japanese insisted upon an American theme park much like the California flagship of which they had grown so

TOKYO DISNEYLAND

fond. With this in mind, Imagineers created themed "lands"—such as Fantasyland, Adventureland and Tomorrowland—that were similar to those in the other parks. Since the concept of the frontier did not translate into Japanese, Westernland was the name given to the area known as Frontierland at Disneyland. Main Street, U.S.A., while looking much the same, was called World Bazaar, and the entire area was covered by an enormous roof due to the region's often inclement weather conditions. The park was to become the most heavily attended of all the Disney theme parks, welcoming an average of 10 million guests per year.

Another first for the Company came only three days after the opening of Tokyo Disneyland when The Disney Channel began broadcasting. The world of cable television was new to Disney, but proved to be a worthwhile venture. The network, which featured a wide array of Disney films, original programming and family-oriented fare, started with 18 hours of programming a day, but a few years later expanded to a full 24 hours.

The Disney Channel began producing a series of made-for-cable original motion pictures known as Disney Channel Premiere Films. The first of these was the baseball fantasy, *Tiger Town.* Three popular series on the Disney Channel were *Mousercise,* a fast-paced aerobics show for families, *Mouseterpiece Theater,* which presented various Disney cartoons hosted by George Plimpton and *Welcome to Pooh Corner,* with life-size puppets of Pooh and his friends

TOKYO DISNEYLAND

MOUSERCISE

THE DISNEY CHANNEL

WELCOME TO POOH CORNER

HORIZONS AT EPCOT CENTER

PINOCCHIO'S DARING JOURNEY

MR. TOAD'S WILD RIDE IN THE NEW FANTASYLAND AT DISNEYLAND

telling stories of friendship, honesty and cooperation.

In EPCOT Center at Walt Disney World, Horizons, the newest Future World pavilion, opened. Horizons was the first pavilion dedicated completely to the future, allowing guests to experience what life might be like in the desert, space and under the sea.

A new Fantasyland opened at Disneyland Park. The medieval fair design of the original Fantasyland was abandoned for elaborately themed facades. While many of the major attractions in Fantasyland were remodelled and refurbished, new attractions such as Pinocchio's Daring Journey and the Sword in the Stone Ceremony also opened. In addition, enormous inflatable characters made their way down Main Street, U.S.A. in the Flights of Fantasy Parade.

The Studio released only three features this year—*Never Cry Wolf*, *Trenchcoat* and *Something Wicked*

UNCLE SCROOGE AND GOOFY IN
MICKEY'S CHRISTMAS CAROL

NEVER CRY WOLF

This Way Comes—the last based on the book by famed science fiction author Ray Bradbury. Also released was *Mickey's Christmas Carol*, based on the classic Charles Dickens story. With Uncle Scrooge as Ebenezer, Mickey Mouse as Bob Cratchit and Goofy as Jacob Marley's ghost, the new animated featurette brought many of Disney's favorite characters back to the silver screen after a far too long absence. 1983 also saw the release of Disney's fourth installment of the "Pooh" films, *Winnie the Pooh and a Day for Eeyore.*

WINNIE THE POOH AND A DAY FOR EEYORE

☆1984

Donald Duck, one of Disney's most universally adored characters, celebrated his fiftieth birthday in 1984. Over the past half century, the feisty fowl starred in 128 of his own cartoons, as well as appearing in numerous shorts with Mickey Mouse, Goofy and Pluto.

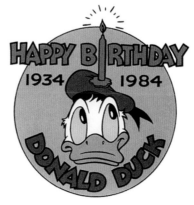

1984 marked the lowest point in numbers of theatrical releases by Walt Disney Productions in three decades. For theater audiences, besides *Splash* and *Country*, there were three reissues, plus the Disney Channel's *Tiger Town*, which was released theatrically only in Detroit to coincide with the World Series.

Frankenweenie, a live-action featurette that paid homage to the great horror films of the 1930s, was released. Directed by Tim Burton and starring Barret Oliver, Shelley Duvall and Daniel Stern, the film is about young Victor Frankenstein who plans to bring his dog, Sparky, back to life after the pup has been hit by a car.

At the theme parks, Morocco opened in EPCOT Center at the Walt Disney World Resort. Morocco was the first pavilion added to World Showcase since the opening of EPCOT Center in 1982, and it was the only one to have its home country as sponsor.

Under the guidance of Walt Disney Productions president Ron Miller, the Studio introduced its second motion picture label, Touchstone Pictures. The new film banner allowed the Studio to produce films for a more mature audience without infringing on the Disney label's family-oriented fare. Touchstone's first film, *Splash*, was released this year, starring Tom Hanks and Daryl Hannah and directed by Ron Howard.

Also produced by Touchstone was *Country*, starring Jessica Lange as a heroic farmer's wife who has to hold her family together while defending the family farm against the government's threat of foreclosure. Lange was nominated for Best Actress by the Academy for her performance.

MOROCCO IN WORLD SHOWCASE AT EPCOT CENTER

Opening at both Disneyland Park and the Magic Kingdom at Walt Disney World was the new Circle-Vision presentation, *American Journeys*. Also opening at both parks was the Country Bear Christmas Special at the Country Bear Jamboree. The new show also marked the first time a major Disney theme park attraction had been changed to present a seasonal program.

The year, however, was a turbulent one at Disney. Twice, investors specializing in corporate takeovers perceived Disney stock as undervalued. They began buying up huge blocks of stock, causing the company to take drastic counter-measures. Walt's nephew, Roy E. Disney, entered the scene to help save the company that his uncle and father had built, from being bought, divided into pieces and sold as some investors had hoped to do. This culminated in the board's decision to ask Michael Eisner and Frank Wells to join Walt Disney Productions as chairman and president.

Prior to joining Disney, Eisner had been a senior vice president at ABC Entertainment and president and chief operating officer of Paramount Pictures Corp., while Wells joined Disney after serving as an executive at Warner Bros. The Eisner-Wells team would be credited with bringing the faltering Disney organization back to its original glory, taking the company to new heights and exploring new avenues in the world of entertainment.

FILMING OF *AMERICAN JOURNEYS* IN CIRCLE-VISION

BIG AL IN THE COUNTRY BEAR CHRISTMAS SPECIAL AT WALT DISNEY WORLD

COUNTRY BEAR CHRISTMAS SPECIAL

FRANK WELLS AND MICHAEL EISNER JOIN WALT DISNEY PRODUCTIONS

SKYFEST AT DISNEYLAND

Disneyland turned 30 in 1985, and the park celebrated by presenting every 30th guest with a special gift from the Gift-Giver Extraordinaire Machine. In addition to the anniversary festivities, Videopolis opened in Fantasyland as a high-tech dancing area that featured hit rock music from contemporary artists. On December 5, Walt Disney's birthday, the city of Anaheim saluted Disneyland with a world-record release of one million balloons, which blanketed the skies above "The Happiest Place on Earth." So much helium was used for Skyfest (70,000 pounds to be exact) that it would have been enough to lift 190 people into the air.

Due to adverse weather conditions in Washington, D.C., the inaugural parade for President Ronald Reagan had to be canceled; instead he attended a special inaugural parade at EPCOT Center.

Walt Disney Television Animation premiered its first two animated tele-

GIFT-GIVER EXTRAORDINAIRE MACHINE AT DISNEYLAND

PRESIDENT AND MRS. REAGAN ATTEND AN
INAUGURAL PARADE AT EPCOT CENTER

vision series in 1985, *Disney's Wuzzles* and *Disney's Adventures of the Gummi Bears*. Touchstone Television introduced its first sitcom, *The Golden Girls*. The hit NBC comedy featured the sultry Blanche Devereaux (Rue McClanahan), the naive Rose Nyland (Betty White), the ever-so-practical Dorothy Zbornak (Bea Arthur) and Sophia Petrillo (Estelle Getty), Dorothy's feisty Sicilian mother. Over the course of the show's seven seasons, the cast and crew would take home an impressive 11 Emmy Awards—more than any other Disney television production.

The Disney Channel premiered a new children's series, *Dumbo's Circus*. With the aid of "puppetronics," the program utilized song, dance, and clever storylines to tell the further adventures of Dumbo and his circus pals.

Also in 1985 Walt Disney Pictures presented *The Journey of Natty Gann*, the story of a 14-year-old girl who hops trains from Chicago to Washington State to be reunited with her lumberjack father. Along the way, she befriends a wolf and a teenage drifter named Harry, played by John Cusack in his first role at Disney. Dorothy Gale once again finds herself in the Emerald City in *Return to Oz*, and an angel named Gideon restores the Christmas spirit to a young mother in *One Magic Christmas*, the first film begun under the new regime at Disney. Meanwhile, released under the new Touchstone Pictures label were two films, *Baby… Secret of the Lost Legend* and *My Science Project*, both of which did modest business at the box office.

(TOP) FAIRUZA BALK IN *RETURN TO OZ;* (ABOVE) TARAN AND EILONWY IN *THE BLACK CAULDRON*

Disney also released its 25th animated feature, *The Black Cauldron*, which was based on Lloyd Alexander's five-volume mythological fantasy, *The Chronicles of Prydain*. In the film, Taran, a valiant young pig keeper, rescues his clairvoyant pig, Hen Wen, from the evil Horned King's castle.

The year also marked a significant financial milestone for Walt Disney Productions, as the company's revenues exceeded $2 billion for the first time.

1986

Richard Dreyfuss and Bette Midler played their first of what would be many roles at Disney in the Touchstone Pictures comedy *Down and Out in Beverly Hills*. The film was the first major feature to come from the new Eisner administration and proved to be a tremendous financial success at the box office. For Dreyfuss and Midler, *Down and Out in Beverly Hills* provided a significant boost to their careers, opening the doors to a variety of roles in films produced by Disney and other studios.

Another set of stars, Paul Newman and Tom Cruise, also starred in their first film with Disney, *The Color of Money*, in which Newman played a retired pool hustler and Cruise played his cocky protege. Newman won his first Academy Award for his performance, earning the Oscar for Best Actor. Touchstone released several other popular comedies this year, such as *Ruthless People, Off Beat* and *Tough Guys*. Under the Walt Disney Pictures label came *Flight of the Navigator*, the story of a boy who assists an alien in navigating his spaceship.

The animated feature *The Great Mouse Detective*, based on the story "Basil of Baker Street" by Eve Titus, was also released, with the dashing Basil rescuing an ingenious toymaker and saving Queen Moustoria's monarchy from the clutches of the evil Ratigan.

PAUL NEWMAN AND TOM CRUISE IN *THE COLOR OF MONEY*

BASIL AND DAWSON IN *THE GREAT MOUSE DETECTIVE*

Disneyland presented the Totally Minnie Parade, and debuted its brand-new summer show, the Country Bear Vacation Hoedown (a reprogrammed version of the original show), at the Country Bear Playhouse. In an effort to boost park attendance in the off-season, the Eisner–Wells administration instituted a new trend of special promotional events at the park, the first of which was Circus Fantasy, an entertainment spectacular held along Main Street, U.S.A., which began in late January.

TOTALLY MINNIE PARADE AT DISNEYLAND

At the Walt Disney World Resort, The Living Seas opened in Future World at Epcot (EPCOT Center had its name simplified). The pavilion was home to the largest saltwater tank in the world (5.7 million gallons), which contained the world's largest man-made coral reef, teeming with manatees, dolphins, tropical fish and other marine life. Opening at Epcot and Disneyland was the 3D musical science fiction adventure film *Captain EO,* starring Michael Jackson.

THE LIVING SEAS
AT EPCOT

The Disney Sunday Movie, featuring classic Disney films and specials, debuted on ABC with Disney CEO Michael Eisner as host. This program signified the return of the Disney anthology show to network television after a three-year absence. Disney also began to produce *Siskel & Ebert,* a program in which Chicago movie critics Gene Siskel and Roger Ebert reviewed the latest Hollywood flicks on their own syndicated television series.

THE GOLF RESORT AT WALT DISNEY WORLD CHANGED ITS NAME TO THE DISNEY INN

The year also marked a major change when Walt Disney Productions received a new name. Since Disney had grown into much more than just a movie studio, with businesses ranging from consumer products and publishing to theme parks and beyond, it was renamed The Walt Disney Company, which seemed to better encompass the varied units of the corporation.

From studio productions to theme parks, 1986 was the first year that the new Disney management team's efforts made a significant impact on the Company's performance. Nearly every division experienced a boost in revenue and activity, a sign that even greater things were on the horizon. Disney was clearly on its way to regaining its status as a major force in the entertainment industry.

☆1987

Disney celebrated the 50th anniversary of *Snow White and the Seven Dwarfs* in 1987 with a series of special events, including a theatrical reissue of the film, a golden anniversary parade at Disneyland and the dedication of a star on the Hollywood Walk of Fame for Walt Disney's first heroine, Snow White.

At the theme parks, Star Tours, a flight simulator attraction based on George Lucas's *Star Wars* films, opened in Tomorrowland at Disneyland Park. This attraction marked the first time an aerospace simulator was used in a theme park; the use of simulators would later become a staple in the theme park industry.

Disneyland introduced Disney Dollars—its exclusive line of currency featuring Mickey Mouse on the $1 bill and Goofy on the $5 bill. The popular Circus Fantasy promotional event returned to the Park for the winter and spring seasons, and State Fair, a new off-season event featuring country fair–style games and booths, debuted in the fall. In other theme park news, an agreement to build Euro Disneyland on the outskirts of Paris was signed in France.

In the movie theaters, Ted Danson, Tom Selleck and Steve Guttenberg were plunged into fatherhood in *Three Men and a Baby*, the first Disney film to exceed the magical $100-million mark at the box office, and Robin Williams would receive a Best Actor Academy Award nomination for his starring role as the irreverent military disc jockey Adrian Cronauer in the hit Touchstone comedy *Good Morning, Vietnam*. *Stakeout*, starring Richard Dreyfuss and Emilio Estevez as intrepid police detectives, and *Outrageous Fortune*, with Shelley Long and Bette Midler playing rivals in romance, were also popular comedies produced by the Studio. The number of feature films produced by Disney grew to ten from seven the previous year.

DISNEY DOLLAR

STATE FAIR AT DISNEYLAND

The tremendously popular animated television series, *DuckTales*, also debuted in 1987. The series followed the daring adventures of Scrooge McDuck, Launchpad McQuack, Webbigail Vanderquack and Huey, Dewey and Louie.

Disney Consumer Products opened its first Disney Store at the Glendale Galleria in California. The new retail store, owned and operated by Disney, sold only Disney-themed merchandise. This first test store would prove to be a highly successful business with hundreds of locations eventually established around the world.

The Walt Disney Company also started the Disney Legends program to honor those whose contributions had made a significant impact on its history. Honorees would put their handprints and signatures in cement in front of the theater at the Disney Studios as a lasting tribute to the men and women who helped make Disney what it is today. Frequent Disney star Fred MacMurray was the first to be honored with the prestigious award.

ROBIN WILLIAMS IN *GOOD MORNING, VIETNAM*

DUCKTALES

WHO FRAMED ROGER RABBIT (©TOUCHSTONE PICTURES AND AMBLIN ENT., INC.)

OLIVER AND DODGER IN *OLIVER & COMPANY*

1988

Disney introduced its newest animated superstar, Roger Rabbit, when it released the Touchstone Pictures/Amblin Entertainment comedy *Who Framed Roger Rabbit* into movie theaters in 1988. For the first time in Hollywood history, Disney's classic characters were teamed up on-screen with animated characters from other studios for a rollicking adventure in the wacky world of toons. It was honored with four Academy Awards, including Film Editing Sound Effects Editing, Visual Effects and an Award for Special Achievement in Animation Direction to Richard Williams.

In other animation news, Disney's *Oliver & Company*, set in New York City, gave a new "twist" to the classic Charles Dickens tale. *Oliver & Company* was the first film produced by

Walt Disney Feature Animation to require an entire production unit responsible for generating computer animation, as seen throughout the film, from cabs and buses to cityscapes and sewer pipes.

Tom Cruise starred in the Touchstone Pictures film *Cocktail*, about an ambitious young man who becomes a talented and popular bartender working out of New York and Jamaica. Bette Midler filled the lead role in *Beaches*, a touching story of friendship and love, and Sidney Poitier played an FBI agent hot on the trail of a ruthless murderer in *Shoot to Kill*.

On TV, Disney produced its first daytime television talk show, *Live with Regis and Kathie Lee*, an entertaining hour-long program which became an instant hit with viewers. The Touchstone Television comedy *Empty Nest*, a spin-off of the *Golden Girls*, debuted. *The New Adven-*

tures of Winnie the Pooh also premiered, starring the cuddly character in his first animated television series. Also in the world of television, Disney acquired its first television station, Los Angeles's KHJ-TV, which would be renamed KCAL in 1989.

In honor of Mickey Mouse's 60th birthday, the Magic Kingdom at Walt Disney World opened Mickey's Birthdayland, its newest themed "land" since the park's opening in 1971. Epcot opened its Norway pavilion in World Showcase with a large stave church as its focal point. The Maelstrom attraction also opened in Norway, taking guests on a voyage through Norwegian history and

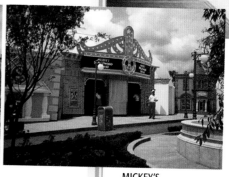

MICKEY'S BIRTHDAYLAND

THE NEW ADVENTURES OF WINNIE THE POOH

MAELSTROM IN
NORWAY AT EPCOT

ILLUMINATIONS IN WORLD SHOWCASE AT EPCOT

(ABOVE) THE GRAND FLORIDIAN BEACH RESORT AT
WALT DISNEY WORLD; (AT LEFT) LOBBY OF THE GRAND
FLORIDIAN

mythology. Also at Epcot, fireworks, lasers and symphonic music filled the nighttime sky with Illuminations, an evening entertainment extravaganza highlighting the countries surrounding the World Showcase Lagoon.

Walt Disney World also opened The Grand Floridian Beach Resort with more than 800 rooms graced with a distinctively Victorian decor. Inspired by San Diego's historic Hotel del Coronado, the Grand Floridian boasted a lobby with dazzling chandeliers, intricate stained glass domes, an open-cage elevator and grand staircases. It also housed Victoria and Albert's, the most exclusive restaurant at Walt Disney World.

At Disneyland Park, in anticipation of the 1989 opening of the Splash Mountain attraction, Bear Country was renamed Critter Country. Disney acquired the Disneyland Hotel from the Wrather Corporation, which had built and operated the hotel since its

QUEEN MARY AND SPRUCE GOOSE IN LONG BEACH

The Walt Disney World Resort enjoyed a banner year in 1989, which was highlighted by the opening of its third theme park—the Disney-MGM Studios, a celebration of Hollywood in its heyday. In addition to being an operating movie studio, the new park opening in 1955. In addition to the hotel, Disney also took over management of the famous ocean liner—the *Queen Mary*—and the Spruce Goose, Howard Hughes's enormous wooden airplane, both located in Long Beach, California.

☆1989

The story of an irrepressible young mermaid named Ariel, who longed for a forbidden life on land, captured the attention of movie audiences around the world, making *The Little Mermaid* the most successful Disney animated feature in decades. It would earn Academy Awards for Best Song ("Under the Sea") and Best Original Score. The film's phenomenal success generated renewed excitement in the animation and musical genres, bringing with it the dawn of a new Golden Age in Disney animation. By the mid 1980s, most of the animators who served under Walt Disney had retired, opening the door to a new generation of artists, and for them, *The Little Mermaid* was just the beginning.

(TOP) ARIEL AND SEBASTIAN IN *THE LITTLE MERMAID;* (MIDDLE) URSULA IN *THE LITTLE MERMAID;* (AT LEFT) DISNEY-MGM STUDIOS GRAND OPENING

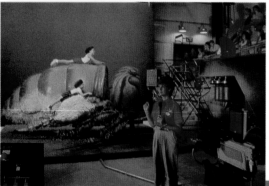

LOOKING DOWN HOLLYWOOD
BLVD. AT DISNEY-MGM STUDIOS

featured its own version of the famed Hollywood Boulevard, including a detailed reproduction of Grauman's Chinese Theater, home of the Great Movie Ride.

THE GREAT MOVIE RIDE

CATASTROPHE
CANYON ON
BACKSTAGE
STUDIO TOUR

Other points of interest included Star Tours, the Indiana Jones® Epic Stunt Spectacular, the Backstage Studio Tour and the Monster Sound Show. Shopping and dining added to the Hollywood experience, with a variety of movie memorabilia at Sid Cahuenga's One-of-a-Kind Shop and themed eateries such as the '50s Prime Time Cafe and the Hollywood Brown Derby, a replica of the restaurant famous for its Cobb salad and grapefruit cake.

BACKSTAGE
STUDIO TOUR

THE HOLLYWOOD BROWN DERBY

DINOSAUR
GERTIE'S ICE
CREAM OF
EXTINCTION

EARFFEL TOWER AT DISNEY-MGM STUDIOS

PLEASURE ISLAND

Also debuting at the Walt Disney World Resort was the nighttime entertainment area, Pleasure Island, which included dance clubs, movie theaters, and restaurants. Epcot opened its newest Future World pavilion, Wonders of Life, featuring the adventurous Body Wars attraction, Cranium Command, and educational films including *Goofy About Health* and *The Making of Me.* In response to the overwhelming popularity of the Resort's first water park, River Country, Typhoon Lagoon was opened, with highlights including Shark Reef, Castaway Creek and the water slide Humunga Kowabunga. Both Walt Disney World and Disneyland Park shared a special milestone in 1989, as each welcomed its 300-millionth guest. While it took Disneyland 34 years to accomplish this feat, it took Walt Disney World less than 18.

BODY WARS

WONDERS OF LIFE AT EPCOT

CASTAWAY CREEK AT TYPHOON LAGOON

At Disneyland Park, the Splash Mountain attraction opened, boasting a harrowing 52-foot flume drop, at the time the world's longest. Based on the animated sequences and characters from *Song of the South,* Splash Mountain followed the adventures of Brer Rabbit as he tries to elude sly Brer Fox and bumbling Brer Bear. Observant guests noticed that many former *Audio-Animatronics* characters from the America Sings

CHIP 'N' DALE'S RESCUE RANGERS

attraction, which closed in 1988, had taken on new roles as part of the Splash Mountain show.

Back at the Disney Studios in Burbank, Touchstone Pictures released the immensely popular film *Dead Poets Society,* starring Robin Williams as a dedicated English teacher who encourages his pupils to "seize the day" and think for themselves. Walt Disney Pictures presented *Honey, I Shrunk the Kids,* a film about a quirky professor named Wayne Szalinski whose children are accidentally reduced to 1/4 inch size by his electromagnetic shrinking machine. Released with it was *Tummy Trouble,* the first Roger Rabbit short produced since the success of *Who Framed Roger Rabbit,* as well as the first animated short produced by the Disney Studio in nearly a quarter century. In total, 11 films, including *Three Fugitives, Disorganized Crime, Turner & Hooch, Cheetah* and *Blaze,* were released by Disney.

On the small screen, the mischievous Chip 'n' Dale returned to television to tackle crimes, injustice, and unsolved mysteries in the animated series *Chip 'n' Dale's Rescue Rangers.* The Disney Channel premiered its award-winning *Great Expectations* three-part film and an updated version of the *Mickey Mouse Club.* However, the latter series focused less on Mickey Mouse and was targeted toward a somewhat older age group—in fact, for the first time, the Mouseketeers no longer wore mouse-ear hats.

⭐1990

The Disney Studios enjoyed another successful year in 1990, releasing 15 new films, including *Pretty Woman*, starring Julia Roberts and Richard Gere; *Three Men and a Little Lady*; *Mr. Destiny*; and *Green Card*. *Pretty Woman* zoomed to the top of the box office charts, becoming, at the time, Disney's highest grossing live-action box office hit, with a total of $178 million domestically.

An all-star cast joined Warren Beatty as he played the legendary police detective in *Dick Tracy*. The film received three Academy Awards: Best Makeup, Best Art Direction/Set Decoration, and Best Song for "Sooner or Later [I Always Get My Man]." Joining Touchstone, Disney's newest motion picture label, Hollywood Pictures, released its first two films, the initial one being the popular thriller *Arachnophobia*, in which a quiet town is infested with a deadly breed of spider.

1990 was also a prolific year in animation, as Disney produced its first sequel to an animated feature—*The Rescuers Down Under*, while the Television Animation division produced its first theatrical feature, *DuckTales: The Movie, Treasure of the Lost Lamp*. Also debuting theatrically were the Mickey Mouse featurette *The Prince and the Pauper* and the Roger Rabbit short *Roller Coaster Rabbit*.

DICK TRACY

HOLLYWOOD PICTURES' FIRST FILM, *ARACHNOPHOBIA*

BERNARD, BIANCA AND JAKE IN *THE RESCUERS DOWN UNDER*

DUCKTALES: THE MOVIE, TREASURE OF THE LOST LAMP

(ABOVE LEFT) *THE PRINCE AND THE PAUPER;* (ABOVE RIGHT) ROGER RABBIT AND BABY HERMAN IN *ROLLER COASTER RABBIT*

Disney proved its commitment to building its television production units with seven new series debuting in 1990. This was, at the time, the highest number of Disney-produced series to premiere in a single year. Some highlights included comedy queen Carol Burnett's return to television on *Carol & Co.* and Dick Clark as the host of *The Challengers*, a syndicated question-and-answer game show. *TaleSpin*, an animated television series starring Baloo, Louie and Kit Cloudkicker, premiered on The Disney Channel, and later became part of the new *Disney Afternoon*, a two-hour syndicated package of animated television series. The first year of *The Disney Afternoon* also included *Duck-Tales*, *The Adventures of the Gummi Bears*, and *Chip 'n' Dale's Rescue Rangers.*

At the theme parks, Disneyland celebrated "35 Years of Magic" with the festive Party Gras parade. At Walt Disney World, four new resort hotels opened near Epcot, including the Yacht and Beach Club Resorts, designed by architect and later Disney Board of Directors member Robert A.M. Stern, and the Swan (opened late the previous year) and Dolphin hotels, designed by architect Michael Graves. Graves was also the architect responsible for the Team Disney Building, housing corporate offices, at the Disney Studios in California. Opening in

HONEY, I SHRUNK THE KIDS ADVENTURE ZONE AT DISNEY-MGM STUDIOS

YACHT CLUB RESORT

WALT DISNEY WORLD SWAN HOTEL

1990, the building featured large statues of the Seven Dwarfs holding up the roof.

Hollywood Records was established by Disney to release mainstream music. The label's first release was the *Arachnophobia* motion picture soundtrack. Also released were albums from recording artists including Queen and The Party, the latter being popular singers from the *Mickey Mouse Club* on The Disney Channel.

TEAM DISNEY BUILDING AT THE WALT DISNEY STUDIOS IN BURBANK

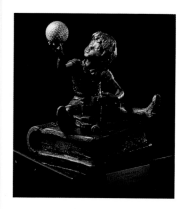

1991

From motion pictures and theme parks to television and publishing, the entire Walt Disney Company was buzzing with activity in 1991. The studio released a record 19 films, with the "Belle" of the box office being *Beauty and the Beast*, a timeless tale of how true beauty is found within. The film's unforgettable characters, including Lumiere, Cogsworth, Mrs. Potts and the self-absorbed Gaston, quickly became some of Disney's most beloved,

And finally, in 1990, the first annual American Teacher Awards was hosted by The Walt Disney Company. The first recipient of the Outstanding Teacher award was Sylvia Anne Washburn.

BEAUTY AND THE BEAST

BELLE AND GASTON

making *Beauty and the Beast* an instant classic. The film made history as the first and only animated feature ever nominated for Best Picture and it earned two Academy Awards, including Best Original Score and Best Song for the title song. *Father of the Bride*, the blockbuster comedy starring Steve Martin as a loving dad who is trying to cope with his daughter's impending wedding, was a hit with audiences, as were films like *The Rocketeer*, *The Doctor*, *White Fang*, *What About Bob?* and *The Marrying Man*.

In television, Disney again smashed its record, premiering 13 new programs, the most notable being the runaway ABC hit comedy *Home Improvement*. With Tim Allen starring as Tim Taylor, the bumbling father and host of the cable show "Tool Time," *Home Improvement* hammered its way into the hearts of families across America. Disney and Jim Henson Associates collaborated to produce

ETHAN HAWKE IN *WHITE FANG*

THE ROCKETEER

DINOSAURS

DARKWING DUCK

MICHAEL EISNER AND ROY E. DISNEY AT
WALT DISNEY WORLD 20TH ANNIVERSARY

WALT DISNEY WORLD 20TH
ANNIVERSARY CEREMONY

SPECTROMAGIC

MICKEY'S NUTCRACKER
AT DISNEYLAND

Dinosaurs, while Walt Disney Tele-vision Animation introduced its newest series, *Darkwing Duck*. Other series produced by Disney included *Blossom*, *Nurses* and *The Torkelsons*.

The Disney Channel began its criti-cally acclaimed *Avonlea* series, which was based on the stories by Lucy Maud Montgomery, author of *Anne of Green Gables*. *Perfect Harmony,* the Disney Channel Premiere Film about two young men at a southern prep school who overcome racial bound-aries to share their love of music, also received wide acclaim.

Walt Disney World celebrated its 20th anniversary in 1991 and began its new fiber optics parade, Spectro-magic, at the Magic Kingdom. The Port Orleans Resort opened at Walt Disney World, as did the Vaca-tion Club Resort, Dis-ney's first time-share hotel facility.

Debuting at Disneyland was the Christmas favo-rite, Mickey's Nutcracker at Videopolis. The stage show featured Mickey, Minnie and all their friends in this classic tale with a Disney twist. And on the international theme park scene, after only eight years, Tokyo Disneyland welcomed its 100-milliionth guest.

Elsewhere at Disney, the Consumer Products division launched its own publishing company, Hyperion, in New York City. Hyperion's library would come to include a wide array of categories, including fiction, bio-graphies, cookbooks, travel guides, sports titles and how-to books, as well as a selection of Disney-themed publications. Another imprint, Disney Press, was created to publish Disney-themed children's books. Walt Disney Home Video released three Disney animated features, Walt Disney's masterpiece *Fantasia, The Jungle Book*

PORT ORLEANS RESORT

VACATION CLUB RESORT

and the *Rescuers Down Under* on video for the first time.

In a year filled with blockbuster films, anniversaries and grand openings, The Walt Disney Company also achieved a significant milestone in the world of finance when it joined the prestigious Dow Jones Industrial Average on May 6.

FANTASIA RELEASED ON VIDEO

☆1992

On April 12, Euro Disneyland (to be renamed Disneyland Paris in 1994), the first Disney theme park in Europe, opened its gates to the public. While Euro Disneyland was similar in layout to the California flagship park, it was referred to by many as the most visually stunning of all the Disney theme parks. Some notable differences existed, the most obvious being the substitution of a

EURO DISNEYLAND

Jules Verne-themed Discoveryland for Tomorrowland. The resort also featured a nighttime entertainment complex originally known as Festival Disney, and six hotels, including the Disneyland Hotel, the first to be located on the grounds of a Disney theme park. Euro Disneyland would eventually become Europe's number-one tourist attraction, even though startup costs originally hindered profit.

The Rivers of America ignited at Disneyland Park with the premiere of its new nighttime entertainment extravaganza, *Fantasmic!*, which featured state-of-the-art pyrotechnics, laser and light effects, a lively musical score and film uniquely projected onto gigantic screens of mist. Elsewhere in the Park, as a special tribute to Goofy during his 60th birthday year, Disneyland presented a special parade, The World According to Goofy.

Walt Disney World, in addition to opening the Old South-themed Dixie Landings Resort, served as host to Disney's first Official Disneyana Convention. While enthusiasts around the world had organized unofficial Disneyana conventions in the past, this marked the first time that The Walt Disney Company itself sponsored such an event.

Among 21 new films, *Honey, I Blew Up the Kid*, the sequel to *Honey, I Shrunk the Kids*, was a hit in movie theaters, as were others such as *Medicine Man*, *The Distinguished Gentleman* and *The Hand That Rocks the Cradle*. An unexpected blockbuster, *Sister Act*, starred Whoopi

WHOOPI GOLDBERG IN *SISTER ACT*

FANTASMIC!

FIRST ANNUAL DISNEYANA CONVENTION AT WALT DISNEY WORLD

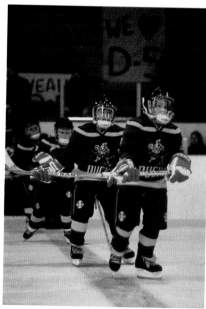

THE MIGHTY DUCKS

Goldberg as a Reno lounge singer turned "singing nun." Disney's *The Mighty Ducks*, the story of a hockey team full of clumsy kids who became champs, was a tremendous success at the box office, and also coincided with Disney's first entry into professional athletics. The Company formed its own National Hockey League team, which it of course named the Mighty Ducks. The team would be based in Anaheim, California, and play at the new Arrowhead Pond.

Disney's Feature Animation division once again hit the mark with movie-goers when it released *Aladdin*. Featuring an amazing comic performance by Robin Williams who provided the voice of the Genie, coupled with an incredible musical selection from Howard Ashman, Alan Menken and Tim Rice, the film quickly became the highest grossing animated feature ever, grossing more than $200 million domestically. It would be honored with Academy Awards for Best Original Score and Best Song, "A Whole New World."

GENIE AND ALADDIN

JASMINE AND ALADDIN

JAFAR

original animation principles to produce a line of meticulously crafted porcelain character sculptures. Characters from *Bambi* were the first to be brought to life through these fine sculptures; surprisingly, one of the most popular was a tiny field mouse reaching for a drop of water.

FIELD MOUSE IN THE WALT DISNEY CLASSICS COLLECTION

On television, Goofy starred in his first animated series, *Goof Troop*, and Ariel made her debut in *Disney's The Little Mermaid*, which was the first animated television series based on a Disney animated feature.

The Company's Buena Vista Home Video division saw *Fantasia* rise to the rank of best-selling video of all time, while Disney Consumer Products launched the Walt Disney Classics Collection, which utilized Disney's

1993

Mickey's Toontown, "the land that toons built," officially opened at Disneyland, making it the newest themed "land" at the Park since Bear Country in 1972. According to legend, Toontown had been located adjacent to Fantasyland for decades, but it was not open to "non-toons" until 1993. Complete with talking mailboxes and manhole covers, the downtown area featured an exploding fireworks factory, an electrifying power company and other zany businesses that only toons would think to patronize. Connected by the wobbly Jolly Trolley, Toontown's residential sector was home to Mickey, Minnie, Goofy, Donald and Chip 'n' Dale.

THE LITTLE MERMAID TELEVISION SERIES

The Studio experienced another busy year in movie theaters, with a record 27 new films released. *Cool Runnings*, the comedic story of the Jamaican bobsled team, was a huge hit for Walt Disney Pictures, as was *Homeward Bound: The Incredible Journey*, a remake of the 1963 Disney live-action film, *The Incredible Journey*. Two of the world's most celebrated holidays—Christmas and Halloween—collided with disastrous results in *Tim Burton's The Nightmare Before Christmas*. Rosie O'Donnell joined Richard Dreyfuss and Emilio Estevez for some slapstick police surveillance antics in *Another Stakeout*, and Kurt Russell and Val Kilmer starred in the immensely popular western *Tombstone*. Chris O'Donnell, Charlie Sheen, Kiefer Sutherland and Oliver Platt were featured as defenders of the King and swooners of women in the swash-buckling adventure *The Three Musketeers*. Other noteworthy films of the year were *What's Love Got to Do with*

HOMEWARD BOUND: THE INCREDIBLE JOURNEY

JACK SKELLINGTON IN *THE NIGHTMARE BEFORE CHRISTMAS*

KURT RUSSELL IN *TOMBSTONE*

CHARLIE SHEEN, KIEFER SUTHERLAND AND OLIVER PLATT IN *THE THREE MUSKETEERS*

ANGELA BASSETT IN *WHAT'S LOVE GOT TO DO WITH IT?*

KIEU CHINH IN *THE JOY LUCK CLUB*

BONKERS

It?, Swing Kids, Sister Act 2: Back in the Habit, Hocus Pocus and *The Joy Luck Club*, a tear-jerking film based on the best-selling book by Amy Tan.

Snow White and the Seven Dwarfs received its eighth reissue in 1993, but this time it was completely restored using digital techniques, the first film to be so restored.

On June 30, 1993 Disney acquired the independent film production house, Miramax Films. From the deal, Disney gained the rights to Miramax's library of more than 200 films and agreed to finance all future Miramax productions.

On television Bill Nye proved to kids that science is fun in his new syndicated television program, *Bill Nye, The Science Guy*. The show demonstrated scientific principles and theories in terms that children could understand and enjoy. Bonkers D. Bobcat fought crime for the Hollywood Police Department's Toon Division in the animated television series *Bonkers*. Ben Savage filled the role of Cory Matthews, a teenager struggling with the challenges of growing up, in the ABC television comedy *Boy Meets World*.

Sadly, on February 16, Sharon M. Disney, the second daughter of Walt and Lillian Disney, died at the age of 57.

☆1994

The highlight of 1994 came on June 24, when *The Lion King* roared into theaters, rapidly becoming the most successful Disney film ever and one of the top ten highest-grossing movies of all time. In the United States alone, *The Lion King* brought in over $312 million in box office receipts. With a voice cast including James Earl Jones, Whoopi Goldberg, Matthew Broderick, Jeremy Irons and Jonathan Taylor Thomas, and music from Elton John and Tim Rice, this coming-of-age story captured the hearts and minds of people around the world. Producer Don Hahn said, "When you're making a movie, you never really know for sure what you're going to end up with. Sometimes we wondered who would want to see a movie about a lion cub who got framed for murder. We just tried to make the best movie we could, and luckily all the planets were in alignment—we had the best actors and the best artists all together in the right place at the right time, and it all worked. *The Lion King* really hit a chord with the audience." The animated feature earned two Academy Awards, Best Original Score and Best Song ("Can You Feel the Love Tonight").

RAFIKI HOLDS BABY SIMBA WHILE MUFASA AND NALA SMILE PROUDLY

PUMBAA, SIMBA AND TIMON

(CLOCKWISE FROM LEFT) TIM ALLEN IN *THE SANTA CLAUSE;* MACKENZIE ASTIN IN *IRON WILL;* RALPH FIENNES IN *QUIZ SHOW;* JASON SCOTT LEE IN *RUDYARD KIPLING'S THE JUNGLE BOOK*

MR. VAN DOREN

Home Improvement's Tim Allen starred in his first full-length feature film at Disney, *The Santa Clause*. Walt Disney Pictures also presented a string of popular films including *Iron Will, Blank Check, D2: The Mighty Ducks, Angels in the Outfield, Rudyard Kipling's The Jungle Book* and *White Fang 2: The Myth of the White Wolf*. In addition, the Studio released *Ed Wood* (which received two Oscars including Best Supporting Actor, Martin Landau, and Best Makeup), *Quiz Show* and *The Ref*. Again breaking its record, the Studio released 29 films this year.

Disney also made its first entry into the theater world with the opening of *Beauty and the Beast: The Broadway Musical* at the Palace Theater in New York City. The Tony Award-winning musical featured several new songs by Tim Rice and Alan Menken, as well as one song, "Human Again," which was written by Menken and his late partner Howard Ashman.

The Walt Disney World Resort was hopping with activity. The Disney-MGM Studios opened Sunset Boulevard, an area filled with themed shops that ultimately led to The Twilight Zone Tower of Terror. Hosted by the legendary Rod Serling, this new attraction took guests on a tour through the remains of a decaying Hollywood hotel, culminating in a horrifying 13-story drop in a runaway service elevator. At Epcot, Communicore was replaced by Innoventions,

which featured virtual reality proto-
types and the latest in technologies
from America's top companies, and
The Legend of the Lion King, which
utilized costumed characters and
puppets to tell the story of Simba,
opened in Fantasyland at the Magic
Kingdom. Several new resort hotels
opened at Walt Disney World as well,
including the rustic Wilderness Lodge
and the moderately priced All Star
Resorts, featuring the All-Star Sports
Resort and the All-Star Music Resort.

SUNSET BLVD. AND TOWER OF
TERROR AT DISNEY-MGM STUDIOS

WILDERNESS
LODGE AT WALT
DISNEY WORLD

ALL-STAR SPORTS RESORT

ALL-STAR MUSIC RESORT

WILDERNESS LODGE LOBBY

THE LION KING CELEBRATION AT DISNEYLAND

ROGER RABBIT'S CAR TOON SPIN

THE FEATURE ANIMATION BUILDING

ALADDIN TELEVISION SERIES

GARGOYLES

The Lion King Celebration parade debuted at Disneyland to streets packed with guests awaiting what became one of the most amazing entertainment experiences ever to run at the Park. Also at Disneyland, Roger Rabbit's Car Toon Spin opened, taking guests on a wild taxi ride through the backstreets and alleys of Mickey's Toontown.

Walt Disney Television Animation introduced two new animated series, *Gargoyles* and *Disney's Aladdin,* while Touchstone Television debuted the hit comedy *Ellen,* starring Ellen DeGeneres, and *Thunder Alley,* starring Ed Asner. On The Disney Channel, *Walt Disney World Inside Out*, a wacky show that explored every facet of both Walt Disney World and Disneyland, premiered.

Buena Vista Home Video released its first direct-to-video sequel to an animated feature, *The Return of Jafar,* which followed the further adventures of Aladdin, Jasmine and the Genie.

In other parts of the Company, Disney Consumer Products formed

Disney Interactive to develop computer games and CD-ROM software, Joe Roth was named chairman of the Walt Disney Motion Picture Group, the new Feature Animation Building, designed by Robert A.M. Stern, opened adjacent to the main studio lot in Burbank and The Disney Stores launched a second retail store chain, The Walt Disney Gallery, which boasted a wide array of Disney collectibles and high-end merchandise.

Despite many successes, on some fronts 1994 was an especially difficult year, and one which would have a tremendous impact on the Company. First came the unexpected death of Disney president Frank G. Wells, who died in a helicopter crash during a ski trip. Wells, who had joined Disney in 1984, worked closely with Michael Eisner, and the two were credited with turning the Disney Studio into a phenomenally successful entertainment conglomerate. In the aftermath of Wells's death, Studio chairman Jeffrey Katzenberg left the company following his unsuccessful bid for Wells's job, and Michael Eisner faced a seri-

ous health scare, which led to open heart surgery. There were also major setbacks on Disney's America, a Virginia theme park concept that was eventually scrapped, and continuing financial problems with Euro Disney. In many respects, things had nowhere to go but up.

1995

Perhaps the most significant event in the history of The Walt Disney Company during 1995 took place on July 31, when Disney announced the acquisition of Capital Cities/ABC. As a result of this $19-billion merger, Disney would add the entire ABC television network, key ABC affiliates, ABC radio networks, publishing enterprises, ESPN, E! Entertainment Television, interest in The History Channel, A&E and Lifetime and much more to its rapidly expanding roster of business units. It seemed fitting for Disney and ABC to come together since the network was a one-third owner of Disneyland when it first opened and had aired Walt Disney's very first television series, *Disneyland*.

Disneyland Park opened its newest and largest attraction, Indiana Jones Adventure: Temple of the Forbidden Eye. Beyond the Park's berm, Disneyland purchased the Pan Pacific Hotel, located adjacent to the Disneyland Hotel, and renamed it the Disneyland Pacific Hotel.

The Magic Kingdom at Walt Disney World reopened its Tomorrowland after a complete renovation, giving

DISNEYLAND PACIFIC HOTEL

WEDDING PAVILION

BLIZZARD BEACH

SPACE MOUNTAIN AT DISNEYLAND PARIS

the area an all-new sci-fi look. Added to the new Tomorrowland was the ExtraTERRORestrial Alien Encounter. The attraction featured an interplanetary teleportation experiment gone awry.

Also opening at Walt Disney World was a third water park, Blizzard Beach, and an ornate Wedding Pavilion was christened near The Grand Floridian Beach Resort. Walt Disney World also announced its intention to build its fourth theme park, Disney's Animal Kingdom, and on October 12, the resort welcomed its 500-millionth guest. In addition, the Disney Vacation Club opened its first location outside of a Disney resort area in Vero Beach, Florida.

Disneyland Paris opened its Space Mountain attraction, joining those at Disneyland, Tokyo Disneyland and the Walt Disney World Magic Kingdom. The Space Mountain at Disneyland Paris was unique, however, as it was the first and only one with an upside-down loop.

The Feature Animation unit presented *Pocahontas*, winning two Academy Awards, including Best

Original Score and Best Song for "Colors of the Wind." The movie was the first Disney animated feature to be based on historical fact, following the adventures of the free-spirited Native American woman who fell deeply in love with the courageous English captain, John Smith. Disney also enjoyed its first collaboration with its new partners at Pixar Animation Studios when it released the world's first fully computer-generated animated feature, *Toy Story*. The film's producer, John Lasseter, was honored by the Academy with a Special Achievement Oscar for "the development and inspired application of techniques that have made possible

(TOP) GOVERNOR RATCLIFFE IN *POCAHONTAS*;
(BELOW) JOHN SMITH AND POCAHONTAS

(AT LEFT) WOODY AND BO PEEP IN *TOY STORY*;
(BELOW) WOODY AND BUZZ LIGHTYEAR

RUNAWAY BRAIN

A GOOFY MOVIE

OPERATION DUMBO DROP

THE LION KING'S TIMON AND PUMBAA TELEVISION SERIES

the first feature-length computer-animated film." *Runaway Brain*, the first Mickey Mouse short in more than four decades, was released with Disney's *A Kid in King Arthur's Court*. And Walt Disney Television Animation produced *A Goofy Movie*, the first full-length film to star the lovable goofball.

Also in theaters, thrill-seekers looked to *Crimson Tide*, starring Gene Hackman and Denzel Washington; hopeless romantics found true love in *While You Were Sleeping*, starring Sandra Bullock; and *Father of the Bride Part II* found the manic George Banks, played by Steve Martin, facing new challenges in fatherhood. *Nixon*, starring Anthony Hopkins in the lead role, was nominated for four Academy Awards.

Also released in theaters were *Operation Dumbo Drop, Dangerous Minds* and *Tom and Huck*. A total of 32 films were released by Disney, once more breaking the Studio's record.

On the small screen, Disney debuted its latest animated television series, *The Lion King's Timon & Pumbaa*, and Belle invited children into her enchanted Book and Music Shop for stories and songs in *Disney's Sing Me a Story: with Belle*. Touchstone Television presented *Brotherly Love*, a new comedy starring real-life brothers Joey, Matthew and Andrew Lawrence.

Disney made its way onto the Internet, forming Disney Online to provide children and families with quality entertainment and information.

☆1996☁

From the Studio's first release of 1996, *Mr. Holland's Opus*, starring Richard Dreyfuss in a touching story about a dedicated high school music teacher, to the last, *Evita*, a musical starring Madonna as the adored Argentine leader Eva Peron (Andrew Lloyd Webber and Tim Rice won the Best Song Oscar for "You Must Love Me"), Disney's film division saw another busy and successful year with a total of 29 films released.

For three of the year's biggest hits, Sean Connery and Nicolas Cage came together to fight renegade military terrorists in *The Rock*, Mel Gibson

EVITA

and Rene Russo took drastic measures to save their son from ruthless kidnappers in *Ransom* and Glenn Close starred as the villainous Cruella De Vil in the live-action film *101 Dalmatians*. *Dalmatians* also broke the world record for box office revenue over the long Thanksgiving Day weekend, raking in an incredible $45 million. For family audiences, Tim Curry joined the motley Muppets crew in their swashbuckling adventure, *Muppet Treasure Island*, while other Disney releases included *Homeward Bound II: Lost in San Francisco, D3: The Mighty Ducks* and *First Kid*, featuring Sinbad as the Secret Service

HOMEWARD BOUND II: LOST IN SAN FRANCISCO

THE MIGHTY DUCKS
TELEVISION SERIES

PONGO AND PERDITA IN
101 DALMATIANS

175

(TOP) QUASIMODO WITH GARGOYLES VICTOR AND HUGO IN *THE HUNCHBACK OF NOTRE DAME;* (ABOVE) FROLLO AND CLOPIN

agent responsible for the president's troublesome son. *The Hunchback of Notre Dame*, a new twist on the classic Victor Hugo novel, was the animated release for the year.

Disney was clearly attracting Hollywood's top talent for its films, including Robin Williams and Bill Cosby in *Jack*, John Travolta in *Phenomenon*, Robert Redford and Michelle Pfeiffer in *Up Close and Personal* and Whitney Houston and Denzel Washington in *The Preacher's Wife*. This applied to animation, too, with Susan Sarandon, Richard Dreyfuss and David Thewlis lending their voices to characters in Henry Selick and Tim Burton's latest stop-motion animation achievement, *James and the Giant Peach*, a story based on the popular children's novel by Roald Dahl.

JAMES AND THE GIANT PEACH

MICHELLE PFEIFFER IN *UP CLOSE AND PERSONAL*

The Walt Disney World Resort celebrated its 25th Anniversary in 1996, with a special ceremony attended by First Lady Hillary Rodham Clinton and Florida Governor Lawton Chiles. Cinderella Castle was transformed into a gigantic birthday cake for the year-long birthday party.

The Walt Disney World Speedway had its grand opening with its inaugural race, the Walt Disney World Indy 200, the new BoardWalk Resort

(TOP) BOARDWALK AT WALT DISNEY WORLD; (ABOVE) WALT DISNEY WORLD SPEEDWAY

opened near Epcot, and World of Disney, the largest Disney merchandise location on Earth, opened at the Disney Village Marketplace.

Celebration, the community adjacent to the Walt Disney World Resort, welcomed its first residents. Designed by Disney, Celebration harkened back to Walt's original concept for EPCOT by providing a community with the latest technologies for the home, as well as the most modern educational and health facilities. The Disney Vacation Club opened another luxury

(ABOVE LEFT) 25TH ANNIVERSARY CASTLE CAKE; (ABOVE) WORLD OF DISNEY AT DISNEY VILLAGE MARKETPLACE

THE HABER FAMILY IS THE FIRST TO MOVE INTO CELEBRATION

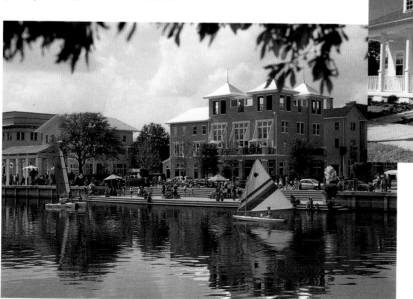

CELEBRATION, FLORIDA

VACATION CLUB AT HILTON HEAD, SOUTH CAROLINA

DISNEY INSTITUTE

THE MAIN STREET ELECTRICAL PARADE HAD ITS FINAL SEASON AT DISNEYLAND

ALADDIN AND THE KING OF THIEVES

resort location in the famous Hilton Head, South Carolina area.

Also opening at the Walt Disney World Resort was The Disney Institute, an educational vacation experience where guests could participate in more than 60 innovative programs.

In other parts of the Company, *Aladdin and the King of Thieves*, the second sequel to the Disney animated feature *Aladdin*, was released on video, with Robin Williams returning as the voice of the Genie. Disney introduced several new animated television series: *Jungle Cubs*, based on the animated feature *The Jungle Book*; *Quack Pack*, giving Donald Duck his first television series; *The Mighty Ducks*; and *Brand Spanking*

JUNGLE CUBS

QUACK PACK

New Doug. Disney Online started its newest venture, Family.com, which provided parents with information on food, travel and family activities. Tokyo Disneyland opened its Toontown and Radio Disney, a new 24-hour radio network for kids, hit the air waves. Disney acquired one of Hollywood's leading special effects companies, Dream Quest Images, as  well as 25 percent of the California Angels major league baseball team from owner Gene Autry. Disney also assumed the role of managing general partner of the Angels.

1997

Hercules, Disney's latest animated feature, told the tale of the legendary Greek hero and his courageous battle against Hades, the evil Lord of the Underworld. The live-action *George of the Jungle,* starring Brendan Fraser,

was based on the popular 1960s cartoon, and was a tremendous hit with audiences. Meanwhile Robin Williams starred in *Flubber,* a remake of the 1961 Disney classic *The Absent-Minded Professor,* and comedian Tim Allen of *Home Improvement* fame played his second role in a Disney film in *Jungle 2 Jungle.* The Studio also presented a remake of the 1965 Disney film *That Darn Cat!*

Other films included *Air Bud,* a story about a basketball-playing Golden Retriever; *Grosse Point Blank,* featuring John Cusack and Dan Aykroyd as rival hit men; *Romy and Michele's High School Reunion* with Lisa Kudrow and

THE MUSES FROM *HERCULES*

HERCULES AND HADES

Mira Sorvino in the title roles; Demi Moore as the first female Navy SEAL in *G.I. Jane*; and Martin Scorsese's film about the Dalai Lama, *Kundun*. Nicolas Cage played an unjustly imprisoned convict who is paroled and hitches a ride on an airplane transporting a group of notorious criminals to a new super-maximum security facility only to have the prisoners take over the plane in the runaway action blockbuster *Con Air*. The Studio released a total of 23 films throughout the year, significantly cutting back on the volume of product.

Disney returned to the Broadway spotlight, starting with the opening of the beautifully restored historic New Amsterdam Theater on New York's 42nd Street. In the fall, *The Lion King*, the most successful animated feature of all time, became a full-scale Broadway musical. The *New York Daily News* called the production "...a perfect marriage of entertainment and art... unlike anything Broadway has ever seen." The show would be honored with six Tony awards, including Best Musical.

THE LION KING ON BROADWAY

The perennial Disney television anthology series, which had taken a seven-year hiatus, returned to the airwaves on ABC under the title of *The Wonderful World of Disney*. Touchstone Television introduced *Soul Man*, a comedy series starring Dan Aykroyd as a not-so-traditional minister, and *Hiller and Diller*, another comedy about a team of television sitcom writers. Also debuting on ABC was *Disney's One Saturday Morning*, a selection of entertaining and educational programs for children. Other animated series produced by Disney were *101 Dalmatians: The Series* and *Nightmare Ned*.

Things were just as busy at the theme parks in 1997. Light Magic, a new nighttime entertainment experience, debuted at Disneyland Park, the Hercules Victory Parade began, and the It's a Small World attraction was decked out for the holiday season, with thousands of lights on the attraction's exterior facade and amazing Christmas decorations from around the world on the inside.

At the Walt Disney World Resort, Downtown Disney West Side opened adjacent to Pleasure Island. The new area featured a Wolfgang Puck restaurant, House of Blues, a Virgin Megastore, Gloria Estefan's Bongos Cuban Cafe and additional AMC movie theaters, among other dining and shopping experiences. Inspired by the grand haciendas of the Spanish Colonial era, Disney's Coronado Springs Resort also opened at Walt Disney World.

NIGHTMARE NED

101 DALMATIANS TELEVISION SERIES

IT'S A SMALL WORLD DRESSED FOR THE HOLIDAY SEASON

LIGHT MAGIC AT DISNEYLAND

DOWNTOWN DISNEY WEST SIDE AT WALT DISNEY WORLD

CORONADO SPRINGS
RESORT

DISNEY'S WIDE WORLD
OF SPORTS

BEAUTY AND THE BEAST: THE ENCHANTED CHRISTMAS

In May, Disney's Wide World of Sports, a state-of-the-art athletic complex with stadiums, fields and fieldhouses that accommodated more than two dozen sports, opened. The facility not only began serving as the spring training site for the Atlanta Braves, but as home to the Amateur Athletic Union and the world-famous Harlem Globetrotters.

Beauty and the Beast: The Enchanted Christmas, the first sequel to the classic Disney animated feature, *Beauty and the Beast*, was released on video just in time for the holiday season. It became a best seller in video stores.

Disney also opened two new flagship businesses in Southern California. The first, Club Disney, was an imaginative play zone and entertainment complex for kids and families, which had its initial location in Thousand Oaks, California. Next was the first ESPN: The Store retail outlet, opening at the Glendale Galleria. The Disney Daily Blast Internet site for kids debuted, the Walt Disney Studios purchased the Mammoth Records Label and Disney Mini Bean Bag Plush toys became the all-time top sellers at The Disney Store.

☆1998

With the gigantic Tree of Life as its centerpiece, Walt Disney World opened its fourth and largest theme park, Disney's Animal Kingdom, on April 22. Spanning 500 acres, Animal Kingdom was billed as "a new species

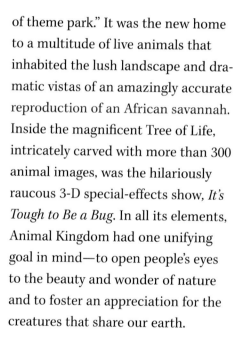

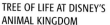
TREE OF LIFE AT DISNEY'S
ANIMAL KINGDOM

ANIMAL CARVINGS ON THE
TREE OF LIFE

of theme park." It was the new home to a multitude of live animals that inhabited the lush landscape and dramatic vistas of an amazingly accurate reproduction of an African savannah. Inside the magnificent Tree of Life, intricately carved with more than 300 animal images, was the hilariously raucous 3-D special-effects show, *It's Tough to Be a Bug*. In all its elements, Animal Kingdom had one unifying goal in mind—to open people's eyes to the beauty and wonder of nature and to foster an appreciation for the creatures that share our earth.

Other new additions were popping up all over the Walt Disney World Resort property. At the Magic Kingdom, Zazu, the hornbill from *The Lion King*, and Iago, the loud-beaked parrot from *Aladdin*, became the new proprietors of The Enchanted Tiki Room—Under New Management, while *Toy Story* superstar Buzz Lightyear enlisted guests in his battle against the evil Emperor Zurg at Buzz Lightyear's Space Ranger Spin in Tomorrowland.

KILIMANJARO SAFARIS AT
DISNEY'S ANIMAL KINGDOM

Elsewhere around Walt Disney World, the innovative, world-renowned acrobatic performers of Cirque du Soleil began an all-new show at their custom-made theater

DISNEYQUEST AT DOWNTOWN DISNEY WEST SIDE

in the heart of Downtown Disney West Side next door to DisneyQuest, a new 100,000-square-foot interactive entertainment/adventure fun zone.

On the opposite coast, on May 22, 1998 Disneyland Park unveiled its highly anticipated, newly renovated Tomorrowland. Representing the futuristic worlds of discovery and imagination inspired by Jules Verne, H.G. Wells and Leonardo da Vinci, the new Tomorrowland's architecture and overall theme heralded a timeless, whimsical fantasy future rather than an attempt at forecasting a "real future" look. The signature attraction was the Astro Orbitor, with its gleaming rockets speeding around a mini-galaxy of rotating planets. Rocket Rods, offering high-speed thrills, replaced the PeopleMover, *Captain EO* gave way to *Honey, I Shrunk the Audience* and the former home of America Sings became Innoventions.

1998's animated feature, *Mulan* was released in June. Based on an ancient Chinese legend, *Mulan* chronicled the daring adventures of a young woman whose irrepressible spirit clashed with her tradition-bound society. *Mulan* was the first Disney animated feature produced primarily by Walt Disney Feature Animation's Florida studio at Walt Disney World.

The year's second animated film came from the creators of the 1995 blockbuster *Toy Story*, as Disney and Pixar Animation Studios teamed up to produce *A Bug's Life*. The film's opening became the largest gross Thanksgiving holiday opening to date.

The most successful film to come out of the Studio in 1998, was Touchstone Pictures' *Armageddon*, which became Disney's highest-grossing live-action film ever, surpassing the previous champ, 1990's *Pretty Woman*. Some of the other releases were *The Parent Trap*, a remake of the classic 1961 Hayley Mills film; *Six Days, Seven Nights*, starring Harrison Ford and Anne Heche; Eddie Murphy as a prophet for profit in *Holy Man*; John Travolta in *A Civil Action*; Oprah Winfrey in *Beloved*; *The Horse Whisperer*, an epic drama directed, produced and starring Robert Redford; and *Mighty Joe*

(TOP) MULAN AND HER FATHER, FA ZHOU; (ABOVE) MULAN AND MUSHU; (AT LEFT) *MULAN* PARADE AT DISNEYLAND; (BELOW) *A BUG'S LIFE*

KIARA, TIMON AND
PUMBAA IN *THE LION
KING II: SIMBA'S PRIDE*

POCAHONTAS II:
JOURNEY TO A NEW
WORLD

Young, in which a 15-foot gorilla from the remote mountains of Central Africa is brought to Los Angeles.

Sequels to two popular Disney animated features, *The Lion King* and *Pocahontas,* had their world premieres on video. *The Lion King II: Simba's Pride* followed the adventures of Simba's daughter Kiara as she struggles to find her place in the "circle of life," while *Pocahontas II: Journey to a New World* took the strong-willed Pocahontas far from her homeland, when she sets sail for the distant city of London on a mission for peace. *Simba's Pride* became the second-best selling video of 1998, bested only by *Titanic,* and the top-selling direct-to-video release of all time.

Touchstone Television added several new series to network television, the most popular being *Felicity* and *Sports Night. Felicity* was the highly anticipated drama starring former Disney Channel Mouseketeer Keri Russell as the title character. A college freshman who follows her heart instead of her parents' wishes, Felicity ends up 3,000 miles away from home, attending college in New York so that she can be close to the boy she had a crush on in high school. *Sports Night,* starring Josh Charles, Peter Krause and Robert Guillaume, revealed the behind-the-scenes mayhem of a nightly cable sports news show.

Also debuting on television was *Disney's Hercules,* an animated series that chronicled the untold stories of the Greek demigod's formative, hero-in-training high school years.

Disney Channel celebrated its 15th anniversary on April 18, and the same day, launched a second cable network, Toon Disney. The new 24-hour all-animation channel showcased Disney's vast library of animation from television series and specials to animated features and classic cartoons. *PB&J Otter*, an imaginative new animated series featuring three energetic otters, Peanut, Baby Butter and Jelly, debuted on Disney Channel.

Eighty-three-thousand tons of luxury ocean liner set sail on the Atlantic when the *Disney Magic*, the first ship from Disney Cruise Line, took its maiden voyage from Port Canaveral, Florida, to Disney's private Bahamian island, Castaway Cay. Celebrating the legendary ocean liners of the 1930s, the breathtaking *Disney Magic* was a modern classic with an elaborately detailed design and luxurious appointments. Castaway Cay, Disney's own private island paradise, offered a vast array of recreational and relaxing activities.

In Baltimore, Disney opened its first ESPN Zone, a location-based entertainment complex that brought together a sports fanatic's two favorite things, professional athletics and lots of food, together under one roof.

In publishing, Walt Disney's biographer Bob Thomas wrote a biography on Walt's brother Roy entitled *Building a Company: Roy O. Disney and the Creation of an Entertainment Empire*, while Michael Eisner's book *Work in Progress*, which told of his years in the entertainment industry, and at Disney in particular, hit bookstands.

Opening in a pre-Broadway tryout in Atlanta was Walt Disney Theatrical Productions' newest musical, *Elaborate Lives: The Legend of Aida*, later renamed simply *Aida*.

1999

In 1999, the Studio's latest animated feature was released. *Tarzan* is a rollicking jungle adventure about a boy who is raised by gorillas. It was based on the classic story by Edgar

THE *DISNEY MAGIC* AT CASTAWAY CAY

TARZAN

TOY STORY 2

ASIA RENDERINGS, DISNEY'S
ANIMAL KINGDOM

Rice Burroughs. The movie featured captivating new songs by Phil Collins, as well as a voice cast including Tony Goldwyn, Glenn Close, Rosie O'Donnell and Minnie Driver.

Woody and Buzz Lightyear, the duo from the 1995 computer-animated blockbuster *Toy Story*, teamed up again when Disney and Pixar Animation Studios collaborated on their third film, *Toy Story 2.*

In Disney's live-action comedy, *Inspector Gadget*, Matthew Broderick brought life to everyone's favorite quirky cartoon detective hero. And Robin Williams starred as an android servant with amazingly human qualities who faithfully serves a family for over two centuries in *Bicentennial Man*. Some of the other films released were *Doug's 1st Movie*, an animated film starring the popular character from the Disney animated television series; *The 13th Warrior* starring Antonio Banderas; Anthony Hopkins and Cuba Gooding Jr. in the drama *Instinct*; Juliette

Lewis and Diane Keaton in the romantic comedy *The Other Sister*; the teen comedy *10 Things I Hate About You*, based on Shakespeare's *Taming of the Shrew*; and *My Favorite Martian* inspired by the classic television series.

At the Walt Disney World Resort, Asia opened in Disney's Animal Kingdom. The new area included the whitewater rafting adventure, Kali River Rapids; and Maharajah Jungle Trek, an exploration experience through ancient temple ruins inhabited by endangered tigers, Komodo dragons and Malayan tapirs. Rock 'n' Roller Coaster, a high-speed music-themed thrill ride aboard a "stretch limo," opened at Disney-MGM Studios, as did *Disney's Doug Live!*, a show starring the animated character, Doug Funnie. At the Magic Kingdom, Mr. Toad's Wild Ride in Fantasyland was replaced with The Many Adventures of Winnie the Pooh, on which guests boarded an oversized "hunny pot" for a journey through the Hundred Acre Wood on a blustery day.

Beginning in the fall, Epcot was the host of Millennium Celebration, a 15-month event featuring grand spectacles, new entertainment and exhibits of breakthrough technologies, all of which highlighted mankind's triumphs, challenges and opportunities. Epcot also saw the opening of a revised Journey into Imagination attraction. Test Track, which gave guests an exhilarating drive in a General Motors test vehicle, took the place of World of Motion at Epcot. It was the longest and fastest Disney theme park attraction, with

a track just under one mile and vehicles that reached speeds of up to 65 miles per hour.

Adjacent to Blizzard Beach, an elf-sized miniature golf course called Disney's Winter Summerland opened, as did the nearby Disney's All-Star Movies Resort.

(TOP) ROCK 'N ROLLER COASTER RENDERING, DISNEY-MGM STUDIOS; (MIDDLE) ALL-STAR MOVIES RESORT AT WALT DISNEY WORLD; (AT LEFT) TEST TRACK

189

MICKEY'S ONCE UPON A CHRISTMAS

MICKEY MOUSEWORKS

Several new animated movies debuted on video, including *Madeline: Lost in Paris*, a film based upon the animated series *Madeline*, and *Mickey's Once Upon a Christmas*, featuring Mickey and the gang in three holiday stories. Mickey Mouse also joined the *Disney's One Saturday Morning* lineup with his first animated series, *Disney's Mickey Mouse-Works*.

At Disneyland, the Swiss Family Tree House was replaced by one featuring Tarzan and his friends from this year's animated feature.

Walt Disney Theatrical Productions opened a stage production of *The Hunchback of Notre Dame* in Germany. The musical was adapted for the stage by Alan Menken and Stephen Schwartz, the same team responsible for the music in the animated feature.

Disney Cruise Line christened its second luxury ocean liner, *Disney Wonder*. Like its sister ship *Disney Magic*, *Disney Wonder* travelled twice weekly between Port Canaveral, Florida, and the Bahamas.

New additions at Disneyland Paris included *Honey, I Shrunk the Audience* in Discoveryland and a Rainforest Cafe in Disney Village.

A major company-wide synergistic initiative began with the January launch of GO Network, an Internet portal site, following the company's 1998 purchase of a major share of Infoseek Corp.

☆2000 AND BEYOND

As Disney faces the year 2000 and the dawn of a new millennium, it is impossible to predict all the changes and advances that will occur within the Company. While there are numerous plans for specific films, theme park attractions, television series and other projects, some are not ready for announcement, and others are simply in the "blue sky" stage, meaning they may happen or they may end up sitting on a shelf forever, never to become a reality. This has always been true at Disney—at any moment, there are literally hundreds of projects in various stages of development. Whether it be Feature Animation, ABC, Touchstone Pictures or Imagineering, eventually the creative minds within the Company's various divisions will review every idea and decide which ones are good enough to receive the "green light" to move into production.

It is certainly possible to take a look at some of the projects that will make their debut in 2000 and beyond because they have already been given the green light, have been officially announced or, as with the parks, are actually under construction.

Fantasia 2000, a continuation of Walt Disney's 1940 masterpiece, will be released in movie theaters in 2000. Walt had always envisioned his *Fantasia* as a constantly evolving piece of art, to which he would regularly add new sequences; however, due to budgetary issues and other production priorities, he was never able to

achieve this dream. Nearly 60 years later, Walt's nephew, Roy E. Disney, spearheaded the effort to realize his uncle's original hope for *Fantasia*, personally supervising the development and production of *Fantasia 2000*. Preceding a traditional theatrical release, *Fantasia 2000* will open in IMAX theaters across the country. This will be the first full-length feature film ever presented in the IMAX format, which has typically been utilized for documentary-style films.

In the world of animation, several new animated feature films are in the works. From the creative minds of John Musker and Ron Clements, the directors of *The Little Mermaid*, *Aladdin* and *Hercules*, will come

(BELOW) "POMP AND CIRCUMSTANCE"; (BOTTOM) VISUAL DEVELOPMENT ARTWORK FROM "KINGDOM IN THE SUN"

CONCEPT ART FOR ANIMATED FEATURE BASED ON THE LOST CIVILIZATION OF ATLANTIS

Disney's first science-fiction animated feature, *Treasure Planet*, an intergalactic version of the classic Robert Louis Stevenson tale, *Treasure Island*. *Beauty and the Beast* and *The Hunchback of Notre Dame* producer Don Hahn and directors Kirk Wise and Gary Trousdale will team up again, this time for a thrilling action-adventure animated feature inspired by the mythological lost continent of Atlantis. Other animated films in various stages of production are *Dinosaur*, the first computer-animated film produced entirely by Disney; *Kingdom in the Sun*, a story based on the ancient Incan civilization; and a new computer-animated film from Disney's partners at Pixar Animation Studios, the makers of *Toy Story* and *A Bug's Life*. Slated for rerelease is a special edition of *Beauty and the Beast*, which will include the newly animated "Human Again" sequence, which had been cut from the original.

Also slated for theatrical release is a new feature film starring Winnie the Pooh and his friends from the Hundred Acre Wood. Additionally, the acclaimed ABC children's series, *Recess*, sparked production on a new animated theatrical feature. A separate slate of films premiering on video include sequels to *The Little Mermaid, Lady and the Tramp* and *The Hunchback of Notre Dame*, as well as *Another Goofy Movie* and the original story *Pirates of the Caribbean*.

In Japan, The Walt Disney Company and Oriental Land Co., Ltd., are building their second theme park, Tokyo

(BELOW LEFT) POOH AND TIGGER MOVIE; (BELOW RIGHT) *LADY & THE TRAMP II: SCAMP'S ADVENTURE*

DisneySea. Set to open in 2001, Tokyo DisneySea will overlook Tokyo Bay and will be adjacent to Tokyo Disneyland Park. The new park will look to the myths, legends and lore of the ocean as the inspiration for its attractions and shows. Inside the park there will be a richly themed luxury hotel, the Tokyo DisneySea Hotel MiraCosta, where guests can actually stay overnight within the park's adventure-filled gates. Complementing Tokyo Disneyland, which has as its foundation the classic Disney stories of dreams, fantasy and magic, Tokyo DisneySea will add a new focus on the imaginative worlds of adventure, romance and discovery, with experiences based on a wealth of oceanic fact and lore.

Opening at Tokyo Disneyland Park in 2001 is the new Fantasyland attraction, Pooh's Hunny Hunt. After boarding five-passenger "hunny pots,"

TOKYO DISNEYSEA

TOKYO DISNEYSEA AQUASPHERE

CARAVAN CAROUSEL AT ARABIAN COAST

LOST RIVER DELTA

CALIFORNIA
ADVENTURE RENDERING

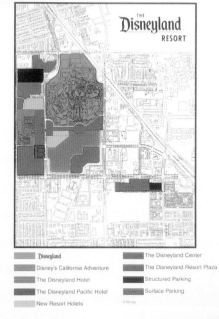

guests will float through an open
storybook and into Pooh's charming
Hundred Acre Wood neighborhood.

At an estimated cost of $1.4 billion, a
major Disney expansion in Southern
California will drastically change the
face of the City of Anaheim. Streets
are being moved and redesigned, free-
way off-ramps are being rerouted and
rebuilt and utilities are being relo-
cated, all to accommodate the most
comprehensive change yet for the
area surrounding Disneyland. Being
built adjacent to Walt Disney's flagship park is Disney's California
Adventure, an ambitious new theme
park project also scheduled to open in
2001. The new park's attractions will
center around the best and brightest
of California, ranging from Hollywood

moviemaking to California's distinctive beach culture to the breathtaking
beauty of the Golden State's scenic
wonders. Besides the new theme park,
there will be a new 750-room deluxe
hotel, the Grand Californian, as well
as a spectacular entertainment center
featuring shopping, theaters and
dining. This entertainment complex,
The Disneyland Center, will connect
Disneyland and Disney's California
Adventure, as well as all three resort
hotels.

Disney's Animal Kingdom Lodge is
slated to open at Walt Disney World
in 2001. The 1,300-room resort hotel
will offer guests balcony views of

CALIFORNIA ADVENTURE RENDERING

194

zebra, giraffe and antelope roaming on an African savannah. Also in 2000, at Disneyland Paris, the Val d'Europe International Mall, a fantastic new shopping experience, will open.

No one can predict exactly what the 21st century has in store for Disney, but one thing is certain: the company is primed to meet the next hundred years by maintaining and expanding upon its presence in all current areas of endeavor, while reaching into some which have not yet even been considered. According to Walt Disney, "In this volatile business of ours, we can ill afford to rest on our laurels, even to pause in retrospect. Times and conditions change so rapidly that we must keep our aim constantly focused on the future."

There is no doubt that through the past 100 years, several generations have been touched by Disney's distinctive brand of creative magic-making. Some may believe that the Disney organization has done all there is to do, but Walt's unending creative vision lives on within the animators, Imagineers, actors, musicians, filmmakers and other employees worldwide who are responsible for paving the road to Disney's future. Just by looking at the projects slated for the first few years of the next millennium, one can see that the future at Disney is both exhilarating and filled with a spirit of fantastic innovation. As Walt once remarked, "A lot of people think the future is closed to them, that everything has been done. This is not so. There are still plenty of avenues to be explored."

GRAND CALIFORNIAN HOTEL RENDERINGS

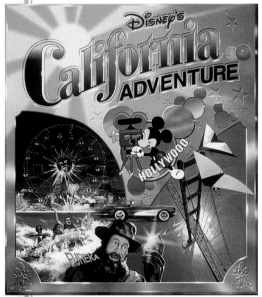

DISNEY'S CALIFORNIA ADVENTURE POSTER

Afterword

BY MICHAEL D. EISNER

From those early *Alice Comedies* and *Steamboat Willie* to *Fantasia*, Disneyland and *The Wonderful World of Disney* to Walt Disney World, *The Lion King, Toy Story* and Disneyland Paris, Disney's first 100 years have seen an explosion of creativity, innovation and imagination that has touched the lives of generations of people here in the United States and around the world.

As we take Disney into the next millennium, we find that the range of entertainment possibilities is greater than ever before. Inside the home, we can reach people through ABC, ESPN, the Disney Channel, Hyperion Books, ESPN Magazine, Disney Interactive and the GO Network. Outside the home, we offer motion pictures, regional entertainment enterprises, Disney stores, Disney ocean liners, theme parks around the world, even sports teams. We are able to move forward in all these established and cutting-edge areas because we have found that the latest entertainment technologies almost always serve to complement and enhance existing technologies. Virtual reality may expand and grow, but it will never replace reality.

As we seize the opportunities that lie ahead, we must never lose sight of one thing: Disney is not simply another company. It is a great American institution that is gifted with a unique heritage all its own. It has the extraordinary power to make us laugh, cry and dream...it has the remarkable ability to bring families together and to forge common bonds among uncommon people around the world. What unusual and distinctive qualities for a corporation! Ours is a company that must always strive for excellence. We must have fun creating fun, while maintaining the discipline to pursue goals that reach for perfection. Guiding us should be a constant awareness that, at our core, we are a silly (Mickey made me say that) little "family" company seeking mostly a simple smile.

I am awed by the many accomplishments of Disney's first 100 years and am excited by the prospect of what the next century will bring. As long as we remain focused, fresh and relevant, I am certain that Disney will continue to amuse and move and inform, regardless of whether people are in their living rooms or local multiplexes, or they are navigating the Internet or the ocean. In this way, we can continue to expand and reinvent this phenomenal enterprise called The Walt Disney Company, while still being true to the roots of the bold and dauntless cartoon studio that Walt and Roy founded back in what will soon be the old century.

Index